FROM PASTA 'PANCAKES
THE ULTIMATE STUDENT COOKBOOK

TIFFANY GOODALL

photography by Claire Peters

CONTENTS

5

BOYS ARE BACK IN TOWN 72

HOW TO Bake a Jacket Potato • Ham and Cheese in Their Jackets • The Classic – Jacket Potato with Beans and Cheese • Saturday Minute Steak Sandwich • Guacamole • Mexican Spicy Tomato Salsa • Hot Tacos • Quesadillas • Fajitas • Sausage and Mash Up • Mashed Potato Variations • Homemade Beef Burgers with Rustic Chips • Hot, Hot Lamb Curry

6

TIFF'S TUESDAYS 88

HOW TO Cook Pizza • Basic Tomato Sauce for Pizza • Pizza Margarita • My Perfect Pizza • Hot and Spicy Pizza • Vegetarian Pasta Heaven • Lasagne • Spaghetti Bolognese • Garlic Bread • Shepherd's Pie • Fish Pie • Thai Fishcakes • Tuscan Chicken Bake

7

WASTED WEEKENDS 108

Perfect Roast Chicken • Gorgeous Gravy • Ingrid's Roast Potatoes • Buttered Broccoli • Gooey Leek Gratin • Beef Stew • Chicken, Bacon and Mushroom Casserole • Lottie's Chicken and Coconut Curry • Fragrant Vegetable Curry • **HOW TO** Cook Rice • Buttered Basmati with Coriander • Thai Fragrant Rice • African Brown Rice • Special Fried Rice

9

TIFF'S TREATS 142

Brilliant Chocolate Brownies • Chocolate Mousse • Apple Crumble • Banana Bread • Cute Cupcakes • Oma's Upside Down Pineapple Cake • Birthday Cake

HOUSE PARTIES 128

Chilli Con Carne • My Ultimate Thai Green Curry • Vodka Watermelon • Cracking Cosmopolitan Cocktail • Sausages • Honey and Mustard Chicken • Lime and Chilli Prawn Kebabs • Barbecued Bananas • The Ultimate Hot Chocolate

BASIC KITCHEN EQUIPMENT

There are so many gadgets and silly machines that try to make basic tasks easier with their ridiculous mechanisms. I am not a fan of squeezy pipettes and general fad gadgets. Just invest in a few great basics.

Saucepans A small saucepan is great for boiling vegetables, eggs, potatoes. A larger one is useful if you are going to cook a soup or a huge stew for a large group. I have a huge one, which is ideal for a large bolognese.

Measuring Jug As cheap as chips yet invaluable, a large plastic measuring jug is not only useful for measuring liquids such as water and stock, but can also be used as an impromptu mixing bowl.

Frying Pan I love a good non-stick frying pan for everything from a good English breakfast to frying mushrooms – it's an essential item and a solid investment. You can buy a thin-edged frying pan that is perfect for pancakes and omelettes.

Colander Brilliant for draining water from pasta, rice, potatoes, vegetables. The list is endless. Plastic and metal versions work equally well.

Wok For the best price and quality, my tip is to go to a Chinese supermarket to buy your wok. They come in handy all the time, from a quick stir-fry to a gorgeous curry. Don't worry if you haven't got a wok, though, a large high-sided frying pan is a perfectly good substitute.

Sieve I tried to live without a sieve as most flours now say 'no need to sieve', however I found myself needing one all the time for all sorts of things, especially when baking, so it's a useful thing to have.

Mixing Bowl I would strongly advise a Pyrex mixing bowl, as it's heatproof. Use it for melting chocolate, cake mixing, making pesto, home-made burgers and whipping up swift salad dressings.

Hand Held Blender I always use a hand held blender. None of the recipes in this book require a food processor. I use this hand held blender for everything from soups to smoothies and cocktails.

Chopping board I am obsessed with thick wooden chopping boards. Some are quite pricey, but if you are savvy you can find them for good prices – just shop around. Plastic works fine too, however.

Potato Masher Brilliant for mashing not only potatoes, but also vegetables such as butternut squash and carrots.

Vegetable Peeler Essential, especially for a roast lunch.

Can Opener Imperative for the kitchen – from cans of beans to tuna, coconut milk and wonderful canned tomatoes.

Grater Brilliant for grating cheese but also great for grating garlic and ginger.

Whisk Even though you can whisk eggs fairly well with a fork a whisk is very handy when making omelettes as it gives them a lovely light texture. More obviously, you'll need a whisk to whip cream or egg whites.

Spatula A plastic spatula is a great implement for scraping up all the leftovers from a mixing bowl. It's also ideal when you need to fold a mixture gently – as with a chocolate mousse. A metal version is useful when you need to lift and drain fried food, such as when cooking a breakfast fry-up.

Wooden Spoon or Spatula These are used extensively in baking. They aren't used as much in savoury cooking as they tend to absorb the flavours and smells of foods such as garlic, onions and chillies. However, they won't scratch the bottom of non-stick saucepans, unlike metal spoons.

Small Fruit Knife One of these makes cutting or slicing fruit or fine vegetables very easy. It's great to have one when making a delicious fruit salad.

Large Knife My large knife is the most useful of my kitchen tools. I use it to chop herbs, meat, garlic, the works.

STORE CUPBOARD INGREDIENTS

It's in here somewhere.

When you are living with family it's easy to take the ingredients that fill up the cupboards completely for granted. However, when you arrive at your university halls of residence in your first year, or your flat or house in subsequent years, there is one thing that is blatantly obvious – the emptiness of the kitchen. The bare shelves and the vacant space in the store cupboards. It's a killer. However, there are a few basic items that you can buy which will keep for ages and serve you well.

Basmati Rice So good with a curry, or to make a lovely special fried rice with bits and bobs in your fridge.

Canned Tomatoes An absolute necessity for any student kitchen, they are used in bolognese, soups, shepherd's pie…

Caster Sugar Used extensively in baking and desserts.

Chicken/Vegetable Stock Cubes A true must have. Used in gravy, soup, risottos, the list is endless. Chicken will be the most useful, but a beef stock cube is also good for hearty red meat casseroles and stews.

Coconut Milk Amazing to have so you can whip up a Thai green curry, or coconut soup with chicken or prawns.

English Mustard Perfect for salad dressings, amazing with mashed potato and as an accompaniment with sausages, burgers, etc.

Garlic Garlic will keep in a cupboard for 2–3 weeks. It can be thrown into all sorts of dishes, from a pasta sauce to a delicious roast chicken. Crushed garlic is seriously potent and a little goes a long way, however, whole garlic cloves can be thrown into a one-pot chicken bake or roast potatoes and they gently exude their flavour.

Ginger This adds a fragrant Thai/Asian feel to dishes. It's delicious in a chicken and coconut curry (see page 120) or a beef noodle stir-fry (see page 69). It's fairly pricey but a big knob goes a long way.

Noodles I love egg and rice noodles, which are great for stir-fries.

YOU WILL NEED:

- Basmati Rice
- Canned Tomatoes
- Caster Sugar
- Chicken/Vegetable Stock Cubes
- Coconut Milk
- English Mustard
- Garlic
- Ginger
- Noodles
- Olive Oil
- Onions
- Pasta
- Plain Flour
- Ready-made Pizza Bases
- Sunflower Oil
- White Wine Vinegar

Olive Oil Great for a lovely dressing or pesto, it is the most used item in my store cupboard.

Onions A must must-have. Buy both red and white varieties; they have a shelf life of 2–3 weeks and should be kept in a dry place so they don't begin to rot.

Pasta A student favourite, pasta makes such a delicious, fast dinner.

Plain Flour Ideal for everyday baking and for thickening sauces and gravy.

Ready-made Pizza Bases Home-made pizzas are epic, and such a laugh to make with your mates.

Sunflower Oil Great for frying, especially breakfast essentials such as sausages, or bacon.

White Wine Vinegar A must-have for salad dressings.

FOOD HYGIENE

Cooking must be fun, as I always say, but you don't want to poison yourself or your mates in the process. Therefore there are a few golden rules.

1 Make sure you have clean hands all the time when you are cooking and wash them after handling raw fish, meat and especially chicken.

2 When handling raw chicken, wash all the equipment that has touched the raw chicken very well. Raw chicken contains very harmful bacteria.

3 When checking to see if chicken is cooked, make sure there are no signs of red and pink and be sure all juices run away totally clear from the meat. Follow all cooking times thoroughly.

4 When reheating a chicken dish, make sure that it is piping hot before you serve it.

5 Do not reheat leftover prawn dishes – discard any leftovers.

6 Make sure that any food stored in the fridge is tightly covered with cling film or foil.

7 Rice cannot be reheated, so eat it all up once you have cooked it.

8 Do not put a hot dish into a cold fridge or freezer as this will cause the temperature of the fridge or freezer to rise. Let it cool down first, then put it in.

9 Make sure a frozen dish is defrosted totally before cooking it again.

1

BREAKFAST WITH TIFFANY

Breakfasts are famously the most important meal of the day – a fact I've found to be especially true while at university. If I start the day with a fresh healthy breakfast, such as a fresh fruit smoothie or fruit salad, I usually feel more like eating healthily as the day goes on too. There are times, however, when only a serious fry-up will do. The traditional Saturday morning fry-up after a heavy Friday night is a must, and I know that my housemates all love the smell of frying bacon. It's amazing how many people discover an appetite at the mention of the words 'fry-up'. And don't underestimate the power of what a good egg can do either. I'm a huge fan and, conveniently, they are also an excellent hangover cure…

BREAKFAST SMOOTHIE SERVES 1

Smoothies are so great for breakfast, and with the recipes here feel free to add any soft fruit you like. Berries work wonderfully, as do bananas, raisins, dried fruit, yoghurts, milk, so go for it and play around.

YOU WILL NEED:
1 banana, sliced
2 tablespoons blueberries
1 tablespoon raspberries or strawberries
2 tablespoons oats or muesli
600ml/1 pint milk

2 Zap it all until all the fruit is crushed and combined with the milk, which usually takes just under 1 minute.

3 Pour into a large glass and enjoy.

1 Bung all the ingredients into a jug where you can whizz them together using a hand held blender.

Leftovers: Drink it straight away as it won't keep for long – your delicious smoothie will soon turn from light pink to nasty brown.

ENERGY SMOOTHIE SERVES 1

This is packed full of energy, as bananas are such a great source of protein. Have this for breakfast and you'll be buzzing all morning.

YOU WILL NEED:
1 banana, sliced
400ml/14fl oz milk
3 tablespoons plain yoghurt, although you could also use flavoured fruit yoghurt

1 Place all your ingredients into a jug where you can whizz them all together with a hand held blender.

3 Pour into a large glass and drink.

2 Blend until the bananas are smooth and combined with the milk and yoghurt.

Leftovers: This will not keep well, as the banana reacts with the oxygen and turns brown, so drink it immediately.

APRICOT SMOOTHIE SERVES 1

Dried fruit is great for your student store cupboard and it lasts longer and is slightly more economical than fresh fruit. It's also readily available at all times. My favourites are dried apricots and I love them like this.

YOU WILL NEED:

110g/4oz dried apricots
1 tablespoon raisins
1 banana
600ml/1pint milk

1 Place all the ingredients in a jug and use a hand held blender to whizz until everything is combined.

2 Pour into a large glass and drink.

Optional Extras: A teaspoon of honey is delicious in this if you have some lying around. Fresh mint is also amazing and turns it into a very zingy summer drink.
Serving Suggestions: Tip some ice cubes into your glass and drink it chilled.

BLUEBERRY YOGHURT SMOOTHIE SERVES 1

The colour of this is amazing and it's so tasty.

YOU WILL NEED:

3 tablespoons blueberries
3 tablespoons plain or fruit
     yoghurt; my favourite is peach
400ml/14fl oz milk

Amazing.

1 Blend all the ingredients in a jug using a hand held whizzer.

2 Tip the smoothie into a glass.

Optional Extras: Whizz in a delicious handful of mixed nuts if you happen to have any.

THE PERFECT POACHED EGG

SERVES 1

YOU WILL NEED:
2 medium eggs
1 slice of bread
1 teaspoon butter

The ultimate poached egg is perfectly runny and soft on the inside – total food heaven. And they're not just for breakfast either. Try one on a salad for a delicious, healthy lunch. Everyone has their own little trick to make poached eggs – I think the key is to use a very fresh egg.

Bring a pan of water to a fast, rolling boil.

2 Meanwhile put your bread into the toaster and butter it when done.

1 Crack your eggs one by one into the saucepan and then reduce the heat to low. Simmer for 4 minutes.

Do this very carefully – you do not want to break them and lose all the delicious yolk.

3 Using a slotted spoon, remove your eggs one by one.

4 Gently place the eggs on your toast. Sprinkle with salt and pepper and eat immediately.

Optional Extras: For pure decadence or for a special occasion, add a tablespoon of hollandaise sauce over the top and serve with bacon. The official name for this is Eggs Benedict. Chopped chives look great, too, and very flash.

BOILED EGG AND SOLDIERS SERVES 1

YOU WILL NEED:
1 medium egg
1 slice of bread
1 teaspoon butter

remember when I had my first hangover after a drunken night at a friend's house; it was my mum who (as mums tend to) knew exactly what I needed, and she whipped up two boiled eggs and soldiers for me in the morning. It was the best meal I've ever had and it hit the spot at the perfect moment. This is a great Sunday night supper too.

3 Drain your egg and place it on a work surface. Hold it in a tea towel as it will be hot. Using a serrated knife, gently cut off the top of the egg and place the rest in an egg cup.

Bring a saucepan of water to the boil.

1 Use a spoon to lower the egg into the pan. Boil for 4–5 minutes for a runny yolk. For a harder yolk cook for 5–6 minutes.

2 Meanwhile toast your bread, spread it with butter and cut it into strips or 'soldiers'.

A bread knife is perfect.

4 Dip your toast in the yolk and enjoy.

Serving Suggestion: You could spoon out all the inside of the egg once it's cooked. Mix it in a bowl with a teaspoon of butter and some salt and pepper, then dip your soldiers in that. Delicious.

Leftovers: A boiled egg will not stay runny and soft for long, but if you are hard boiling them, you can keep them in the fridge, covered in cold water, for up to 2 days. It takes about 8 minutes to hard boil an egg. Use them for egg and mayo sandwiches (see page 49). Great for taking into uni for lunch. Just peel the shell off the egg, grate the egg into a bowl, add some mayonnaise, salt and pepper and put into a sandwich with some cress for tradition, or just lettuce.

SCRAMBLED EGGS ON TOAST **SERVES 1**

Scrambled eggs are a cheap and simple meal. I often have them for dinner with some chopped up ham stirred in. If I'm being decadent I have some smoked salmon with them – that's pretty rare though.

YOU WILL NEED:
2 medium eggs
30ml/1fl oz milk
1 tablespoon butter
1 teaspoon vegetable oil
slice of bread

1 Beat the eggs and add the milk, mix well and season with some salt and pepper.

2 Melt the butter in a pan over a medium heat. Pour in the egg and milk mixture and turn the heat down to low-medium.

3 Keep stirring the eggs all the time. As the mixture heats up, it'll start to scramble. Stir well to stop the lumps becoming too big.

Perfect breakfast.

4 Toast the bread and tip the scrambled eggs on top. Season with pepper.

Optional Extras: For a serious treat, smoked salmon is the ultimate partner to scrambled eggs.
Serving Suggestions: For me it's perfect on toast with a simple squirt of ketchup.
Leftovers: Not great kept in the fridge, so eat up.

EGGY BREAD WITH MAPLE SYRUP

SERVES 1

This is what I feasted on during my childhood – totally delicious and so easy to make. These days it's a favourite Sunday morning breakfast. The French call it *pain perdu*; bread soaked in milk and served fried with maple syrup or honey. It works even better when made with bread that's a day or two old – ideal for most student kitchens.

YOU WILL NEED:

300ml/10fl oz milk
2 medium eggs, beaten
2 slices of bread
1 tablespoon butter
1 tablespoon maple syrup or runny honey

2 Dip the bread in the mixture, slice by slice, and leave to soak for a minute to absorb the milk and egg. By the time you have done both slices most of the mixture should have been absorbed.

1 Mix the milk and beaten eggs together in a shallow dish.

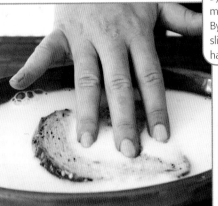

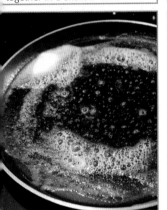

3 Melt the butter in a frying pan set over a high heat. Once the butter has melted reduce the heat to medium.

4 Add the bread and fry it for 3–4 minutes on each side until golden brown.

Delish...

5 Serve hot drizzled with some maple syrup or runny honey.

Optional Extras: I often use a drop of vanilla essence in the egg and milk mixture; however, it is quite expensive, but if you want to and can afford it, it's great to have in the cupboard.
Serving Suggestions: As mentioned above, this is delicious with lots of maple syrup and honey, but it's also almost imperative to have a rasher or two of bacon which can be fried off in the same pan used for cooking the bread.
Leftovers: Not great to keep in the fridge, so if you have leftovers just go for it and eat them.

JIM'S FRIED BREAKFAST

SERVES 1

My old friend Jim and I met when we were 17. He always begged for a full fry-up after a night out; I went on to realise this was a standard lad's request after a night out. A full fry-up is one of the toughest meals to create perfectly, but the secret is a warm oven. It's the timing that can get you in a tizz, but if one thing is ready before the rest, just put it in the oven to keep warm while the rest cooks.

YOU WILL NEED:
- 1 tablespoon vegetable oil
- 2 sausages
- 2 rashers of bacon
- 75g/3oz mushrooms, sliced
- 1 tomato, halved
- pinch of sugar
- 1 teaspoon butter
- 1 egg
- slice of bread

Preheat the oven to 140°C/275°F/Gas Mark 1.

1 Pour the oil into a frying pan and when it's hot and smoking, add the sausages. Fry them for 7–8 minutes, turning occasionally.

2 Add the bacon and cook for another 2 minutes.

3 Next add the mushrooms and tomato halves, flesh side down.

4 Keep turning the sausages, bacon and mushrooms.

5 Flip the tomatoes and season them with a pinch of sugar, and some salt and pepper.

6 After 5–6 minutes the mushrooms should be nice and golden, and the meat cooked. The tomatoes will be soft and cooked right through.

After 2–3 minutes the egg should become white around the edges.

7 Transfer everything to a plate and put it in the oven to keep warm while you fry the eggs.

8 Melt the butter in the frying pan, then tip in the egg. Do this gently so you keep the yolk whole.

9 Sprinkle with a little salt and pepper and, 1 minute later, use a spatula to lift it out of the pan.

10 Toast the bread and serve with the rest of the fry-up.

Optional Extras: Black or white pudding: fry these for 2–3 minutes in the same pan as the sausages if you're keen. A poached egg (see page 12), a scrambled egg (see page 14) or even a boiled egg (see page 13) can take the place of the fried egg. Fried bread is bread fried in oil and could be tasty. Also if you have any mashed potato lying around, that can taste good fried and served as part of a big brunch.

Serving Suggestions: Serve with a slice of toast and a good cup of tea.

Leftovers: If you have leftover sausages you can warm them up in a pan or in the oven for 10 minutes. Eat them with mashed potato, or in a sandwich or just cold as a snack for lunch. Leftover sausages and bacon will keep in the fridge for 3 days. Fried mushrooms will also keep in the fridge for 2–3 days and can be warmed up in a saucepan on a low heat and served with pasta or alongside a chicken dish.

FRESH FRUIT SALAD

SERVES 5

In considerable contrast to a full fry-up, this is nutritious and so easy to put together with really any fruit you might have lying around. If you make a big fruit salad at the start of the week, and keep it covered in the fridge, it's perfect to tuck into for brekkie or even after dinner. It could also be great taken into uni as a snack. It's totally up to you what fruit you use, but make sure that most of it is ripe otherwise it will not taste as good and will be tough to peel and chop. Be aware, however, that bananas tend to go brown and mushy.

YOU WILL NEED:

1 ripe melon, quartered, peeled deseeded and cut into chunks

1 pineapple, cut into chunks, or use the canned version

2 kiwis, peeled and chopped

2 apples, peeled, cored and chopped

2 pears, peeled, deseeded and chopped

2 tablespoons blueberries

2 tablespoons raspberries

200ml/7fl oz orange juice

1 Combine the melon and pineapple, kiwis, apples and pears in a large bowl.

2 Carefully add the blueberries and raspberries

4 Mix carefully and keep in the fridge until needed.

3 Pour in the orange juice.

Optional Extras: If there's any fruit you want to add or take out then go for it. The orange juice keeps it fresh. A couple of mint leaves and a sprinkle of sugar could always be added.

Serving Suggestions: For breakfast I love fruit salad on some yoghurt or even on cereal. As a pudding it's sensational and very light, perfect with some vanilla ice cream or even some softly whipped cream, and you could even stir through some chopped mint too.

Leftovers: This will keep in the fridge for 4–5 days if tightly covered, although it depends on what fruit you use; for example, bananas do not keep for long at all.

PORRIDGE MAD SERVES 1

YOU WILL NEED:

350ml/12fl oz milk

60g/2½oz porridge oats

1 tablespoon honey

I am officially porridge mad and it's so, so good for you. It's probably the breakfast I have the most, as it's easy and keeps me full all day. Lots of my mates at uni have it for breakfast too and it's great either on its own or with a spoonful of honey.

1 Pour the milk into a saucepan and add the oats.

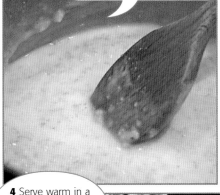

2 As the milk starts bubbling after a few minutes, keep stirring and the oats should expand and start absorbing the milk.

3 It should be ready after 5–6 minutes. If it's too thick add some more milk and if it's too runny add more oats and cook for a few minutes longer.

4 Serve warm in a bowl and trickle over the honey.

Optional Extras: You could add a handful of raisins at the beginning, or a tablespoon of sugar for added sweetness; however, the honey is very sweet. Golden syrup would also be delicious instead of honey.

Serving Suggestions: Lovely with some fresh fruit and some brown sugar sprinkled on top. Lots of people like their porridge with a spoonful of strawberry jam stirred in.

Leftovers: Not so great when reheated, so try and eat it all.

HOW TO COOK PANCAKES
MAKES 4

I get so excited and love the whole experience of making pancakes. It's high time we made more of them! They are ideal for breakfast – quick to make and guaranteed to give you lots of energy for the day ahead. Make a good batter, leave it to rest, make sure you use a good non-stick frying pan with lots of delicious fillings ready and then offer some to your housemates, if you're feeling generous.

YOU WILL NEED:
- 200g/6oz plain flour
- 2 large eggs
- 600ml/1 pint milk
- ½ tablespoon sugar (for sweet pancakes)
- ½ teaspoon salt (for savoury pancakes)
- 100g/3½oz butter (25g/1oz butter per pancake)

If you have a hand-held whizzer you can use it to make the batter extra smooth.

1 Sieve the plain flour in a large mixing bowl and make a well in the centre of the flour. Break the eggs into the well then add the milk.

2 Whisk well, making sure there are no lumps.

3 Add ½ teaspoon of salt if you're making savoury pancakes or ½ tablespoon of sugar if you're making sweet pancakes. If you want your batter to make both types, just leave any salt or sugar out of it completely.

You can use a spatula if you're feeling nervous

5 Swirl the batter to the edges of the pan and then return it to the heat for 1 minute to cook.

6 Flip the pancake over and then cook for 1 minute more.

4 Melt 50g/2oz butter in a non-stick frying pan over a medium heat. Add a ladleful of batter.

7 Tip onto a plate and add the filling of your choice. Repeat with the rest of the pancake batter. If you're making a lot keep them separated by sheets of greaseproof paper and keep warm in the oven at its lowest setting.

Optional Extras: If you're making a batch of savoury pancakes, add some chopped herbs to the batter to brighten it up.
Serving Suggestions: Fill with a whole variety of fillings, such as ham and cheese, cheese and mushrooms, lemon and sugar, chocolate and banana, banana and ice cream…
Leftovers: You can make the batter and keep it covered in the fridge for 2 days, but it's best used on the same day.

HAM AND CHEESE PANCAKES MAKES 4

These pancakes remind me of trips to France – the French cook them to perfection.

YOU WILL NEED:
200g/6oz plain flour
2 large eggs
600ml/1 pint milk
½ teaspoon salt
100g/3½oz butter (25g/1oz butter per pancake)
350g/12oz ham, sliced
110g/4oz Cheddar cheese, grated

1 Make your pancake batter (see opposite).

4 Sprinkle in some cheese and ham

2 Melt 50g/2oz butter in a non-stick frying pan over a medium heat. Add a ladleful of batter.

3 Swirl the mixture evenly around the pan.

5 After a minute, use a spatula to flip the pancake in half, and cook for a further minute.

The cheese will become really gooey and gorgeous.

Tip onto a plate and eat immediately.

Optional Extras: You could add some tomato and a few herbs, such as parsley or coriander, at the same time as the ham and cheese. Mushrooms would also be great. Fry them for 2–3 minutes before adding them to the pancake.
Serving Suggestions: If you're in a hurry, wrap it in foil for a breakfast on the move.
Leftovers: Don't try to keep any cooked pancakes in the fridge as they'll become soggy. If you have leftover batter just keep it covered in the fridge for up to 2 days.

BASIC SWEET PANCAKES MAKES 4

These are sweet, but not too sweet, allowing you to have lots and lots of them. Delicious.

YOU WILL NEED:
200g/6oz plain flour
2 large eggs
600ml/1 pint milk
4½ tablespoons sugar
100g/3½oz butter (25g/1oz
    butter per pancake)
juice of 2 lemons

1 Make your pancakes (see page 20).

2 Tip your pancakes onto a plate.

3 Squeeze lemon juice over each pancake and then sprinkle with 1 tablespoon of sugar.

Ouch!

4 Roll up each pancake and tuck in.

Optional Extras: A drizzle of honey could be so delicious here, or a spoonful of plain yoghurt.
Serving Suggestions: Perfect just as they are.
Leftovers: Keep the batter in the fridge, covered, for up to 2 days.

DECADENT CHOCOLATE AND BANANA PANCAKES MAKES 4

YOU WILL NEED:
200g/6oz plain flour
2 large eggs
600ml/1 pint milk
½ tablespoon sugar
100g/3½oz butter (25g/1oz butter per pancake)
110g/4oz chocolate spread
2 bananas, sliced

The combination of chocolate and banana in a hot pancake is unbeatable. Perfect to get everyone in the party mood. In the summer throw in a few red berries and it's a whole new story.

1 Make your pancakes (see page 20).

2 Tip out onto a plate.

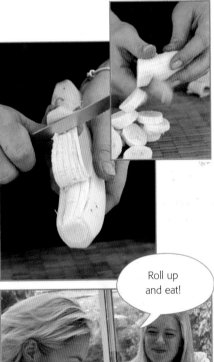

3 Spread each pancake with 2 tablespoons of chocolate spread.

Use half a banana per pancake

Roll up and eat!

4 Sprinkle with banana slices.

Optional Extras: Some chopped fresh mint would be gorgeous here, as would some mini marshmallows, raspberries, or strawberries.

Serving Suggestions: I am a huge fan of chocolate and strawberries or raspberries, so I'd quite like a few of those in my pancake, too.

Leftovers: Keep any leftover batter, covered, in the fridge for up to 2 days.

2 REAL FAST FOOD

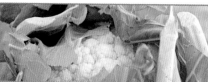

Life at university is fast and furious. Whether facing a long day of lectures, or rushing to get out of the house for a night out, time is always of the essence. This is where this chapter can help, as it shows how to throw a few basics together for maximum results. All the recipes serve one, perfect for weeknight suppers when everyone is busy doing their own thing. Pasta is a reliably great option, and it's always tasty. I've included a few omelette ideas too, as they're so quick, cheap and versatile. Just throw in whatever you have – ham, tomato, cheese… Another economical yet delicious option, risotto, is perfect for mid-week suppers. Plus it has the bonus, as you stir away, of leaving you with one hand free for a drink.

HOW TO COOK PASTA

SERVES 1

Pasta is a key ingredient in the kitchen at university, partly because it's ideal hangover food. An ultra delicious pasta dish can be put together in a very short space of time – just what you need after a long day. It's cheap to buy and dried pasta can be kept in your student store cupboard for a long time. However, like so much in life, it can be the simplest things that can be hardest to get right. So here are a few tips and ideas that I find helpful whenever I'm cooking pasta.

YOU WILL NEED:

1 litre/1¾ pints boiling water
pinch of salt
½ teaspoon olive oil
150g/5oz dried pasta, such as spaghetti, penne, or pasta shells

Pasta is cooked in a big pan of salted boiling water with the lid off. A drop of olive oil helps the pasta to stay loose and not stick together. Dried pasta is cooked for around 9–12 minutes; the packet will show the ideal time for the type you've bought. Fresh pasta cooks much faster, usually 2–4 minutes. Dried pasta is cheaper and keeps for longer though, so is usually better for student kitchens. One more thing to remember: hot pasta waits for no one, so eat it immediately.

1 Bring the water to the boil and add the salt and the olive oil.

2 Add the pasta and stir once to stop it sticking together.

3 The pasta will usually take between 9 and 12 minutes to cook, depending on its size and shape. The packet will tell you how long to cook it, but test it before you drain it by giving it a taste. It will be ready when it's soft, however I like mine when it still has a bit of bite to it.

4 Drain the pasta in a colander and serve it with a sauce of your choice. How quick and easy!

TOMATO AND GARLIC SAUCE

SERVES 1

This is a very basic tasty pasta sauce, but if you want to spice it up there are plenty of options. See my list of optional extras, below, for a few ideas of what you could put in the sauce to make it even more delicious.

YOU WILL NEED:

250g/9oz canned chopped tomatoes

½ red chilli, deseeded and chopped

2 garlic cloves, peeled and crushed

½ teaspoon sugar

1 Begin cooking your pasta (see opposite).

4 Drain your cooked pasta and stir it into the sauce.

2 Put all the sauce ingredients in a pan over a medium heat.

3 When the sauce is bubbling slowly, season it with salt and pepper.

This dish couldn't be quicker and the chilli gives it a cheeky kick. A bit of grated cheese and black pepper on top would finish it off perfectly.

Optional Extras: Try adding any or all of the following to the basic tomato and garlic sauce: bacon bits, mushrooms, finely chopped red peppers, chopped basil, chopped parsley, 1 tablespoon white or red wine.

Serving Suggestions: Delicious on pasta with some grated cheese or with some fresh basil and a green salad.

Leftovers: This sauce will freeze very well, and will keep in the fridge for 2–3 days. If you have any leftovers, spoon them onto some pitta bread, a slice of ciabatta or toast with some cheese and ham and you have a sort of mini pizza. It would also be a great base for a tomato soup; just add around 500ml/18fl oz of vegetable or chicken stock.

MAGIC MUSHROOM SAUCE
SERVES 1

This is so simple yet full of flavour. I use crème fraîche as it's a healthy alternative to cream, but if you have some cream you can easily use that instead. It's perfect with pasta and you can whip this up while your pasta is boiling. In 10 minutes you have a filling supper.

YOU WILL NEED:

75g/3oz butter
1 spring onion, chopped
1 garlic clove, peeled and crushed
75g/3oz mushrooms, sliced
1 tablespoon olive oil (optional)
1–2 tablespoons crème fraîche
1 lemon, quartered
handful of chopped chives
  (optional)

1 Cook your pasta (see page 26).

2 Melt the butter in a pan set over a low heat. Add the spring onion and garlic and cook for 5 minutes until they are soft.

3 Up the heat and add the mushrooms. If they start to look a little dry add a splash of olive oil. When the mushrooms have become soft, add some salt and pepper.

Keep tasting the sauce until you're happy with the amount of lemon juice in it – it should have a citrus kick, but not too much.

4 Lower the heat and add the crème fraîche.

5 Squeeze in some of the juice from the lemon quarters.

6 Drain the pasta, then serve with the sauce spooned over. Scatter with chives, if you like, and tuck in.

Optional Extras: Herbs with this are delicious, so if you have any lying around add them. My first choice would be some chopped chives or coriander.
Leftovers: Any leftover sauce can be kept in the fridge until the next day; I wouldn't recommend any longer as the recipe contains dairy products and these go off quickly. Instead of eating it with pasta again, it would be delicious gently reheated and served on toast or a bagel. Alternatively serve the leftover sauce in a jacket potato – true comfort food.

MA'S CARBONARA SAUCE SERVES 1

My mother makes the most delicious carbonara sauce – creamy, garlicky and truly delicious! The ingredients are basic: eggs, cream and milk are items I often find lying around in my fridge.

YOU WILL NEED:

15ml/1 tablespoon olive oil

2 garlic cloves, peeled and crushed

100g/3½oz unsmoked bacon lardons or normal bacon, chopped roughly

1 medium egg, whisked

2 tablespoons grated Cheddar cheese

125ml/4fl oz double cream

15ml/1 tablespoon milk

1 Cook your pasta (see page 26).

Set your dirty frying pan aside for later.

3 Tip the bacon onto a piece of kitchen paper to drain.

2 Heat the olive oil in a large frying pan, and add the garlic and bacon. Cook over a medium heat for 5 minutes until the bacon is brown, stirring regularly.

4 Mix up the egg, bacon, cheese, cream and milk, and season with salt and pepper. Stir well.

5 Check your pasta and when it's ready, drain it and tip it into the large frying pan you used earlier. Add the egg mixture and gently heat it for 1 minute over a low-medium heat. This is very important because if the heat is too high you will end up with scrambled eggs!

6 Taste to check the seasoning and then serve.

Optional Extras: Flat-leaf parsley would be tasty, chopped and scattered over the top.
Serving Suggestion: A very simple green salad is great with this, as it can be quite rich and the lettuce just mellows it all.
Leftovers: If you have any leftover sauce, it can be kept it in the fridge until the following day. Reheat it slowly in a pan, adding 1 teaspoon cream to make it a little less dry.

BASIL, GARLIC, FETA, ROCKET AND OLIVE OIL SPAGHETTI SERVES 1

YOU WILL NEED:

3 tablespoons olive oil

2 tomatoes, sliced

150g/5oz dried spaghetti

2 garlic cloves, peeled and chopped finely

2 tablespoons roughly chopped basil

110g/4oz feta cheese, crumbled

handful of rocket or lettuce leaves

I came up with this once while looking in the fridge and stuck for what to have for dinner. Lying around in my typically untidy student fridge were some garlic, feta cheese, rocket leaves, tomatoes and some basil, so I put it all together as a sauce with some olive oil, served it with spaghetti and wow, it's now one of my staple and favourite dishes. The handy thing about this dish is you can substitute ingredients for what YOU have in your fridge. So if you have some peppers or parsley, chuck them in. Similarly Cheddar or goat's cheese would work well instead of feta.

Preheat the oven to 180°C/350°F/ Gas Mark 4.

3 Drain the pasta and tip it back into the pan. Add the garlic and basil mixture.

1 Pour 1 tablespoon of the oil over the tomatoes in an ovenproof dish. Put in the oven for 10 minutes.

2 Cook your pasta (see page 26). Meanwhile put the garlic and basil into a bowl, add the remaining 2 tablespoons of olive oil and mix.

4 Remove the tomatoes from the oven.

5 Tip the pasta into a bowl and add the hot tomatoes. Mix well and lots of tomato juice should come out of them.

6 Add the crumbled feta cheese and season with some salt and pepper.

7 Serve scattered with the rocket leaves. Eat immediately.

Optional Extras: There isn't really a limit with something like this. Peppers would be great, any kind of cheese, chives, coriander, canned tomatoes, chilli, bacon… Feel free to go right ahead and add whatever you like.

Serving Suggestions: As you have your salad leaves on top, there is no need to mess around with a side salad, just have a glass of wine or a beer and go for it.

Leftovers: This will keep in the fridge for a day. Warm it up the following day in a saucepan set over a low-medium heat, adding another tablespoon of olive oil. I think it's best eaten immediately though, so eat up.

MUSHROOM AND RED ONION RISOTTO
SERVES 1

Risotto is one of my real favourite dishes to cook, let alone eat. It takes about 15–20 minutes to make and you can let yourself unwind as you monotonously stir your risotto and watch it become creamier and creamier. If you can master a risotto, which is very simple to make, you are on to a real winner. It's great to whack in whatever you fancy, anything from goat's cheese to mushrooms. If you decide to cook some for friends, you'll be surprised how many will be quietly impressed.

YOU WILL NEED:
- 250ml/9fl oz water
- 2 vegetable stock cubes
- 50g/2oz butter
- 2 garlic cloves, peeled and chopped finely
- ½ red onion, peeled and chopped finely
- 75g/3oz arborio rice
- ½ glass of white wine (optional)
- 75g/3oz mushrooms, sliced
- 2 tablespoons grated Parmesan cheese
- handful of rocket leaves

1 Boil the water in a pan then crumble in your stock cubes. Reduce the heat to low and keep the stock simmering while you make the risotto.

2 In a frying pan, melt the butter over a low-medium heat.

3 Add the garlic and the onion. Reduce the heat to low and cook for 5 minutes until the onion is nice and soft.

5 Stir well so the rice soaks up all the delicious melted butter, onion and garlic. Next add the wine, if you're using it.

4 Increase the heat to medium-high and add the rice.

Stir all the time to stop the rice sticking to the bottom of the pan.

8 This process should take 15–20 minutes. Keep tasting your risotto until it becomes deliciously creamy but still with a little bite to it.

6 When the wine has been absorbed by the rice add a ladleful of stock and a pinch of salt.

7 Add the mushrooms and stir. Once each ladle of stock has been absorbed, add another.

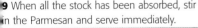

9 When all the stock has been absorbed, stir in the Parmesan and serve immediately.

Some rocket leaves and grated Parmesan would be ideal as an accompaniment.

Optional Extras: This is a very basic risotto recipe using just mushrooms, however you could also add herbs, such as rosemary, thyme (delicious in this), parsley or even chives. A little bacon tastes amazing in a risotto, too. Really the choice is yours. If you don't want to use a red onion or don't have one then a white onion works just as well. I just love the flavour of red onion in risotto.

Serving Suggestions: Risotto is often quite rich, so a handful of rocket leaves really complements it.

Leftovers: Risotto is best eaten immediately, as rice shouldn't be reheated. A great excuse to eat it all up!

GOAT'S CHEESE AND ROSEMARY RISOTTO SERVES 1

YOU WILL NEED:

250ml/9fl oz water

2 vegetable stock cubes

50g/2oz butter

2 garlic cloves, peeled and chopped finely

½ red onion, peeled and chopped finely

75g/3oz arborio rice

1 sprig of rosemary, chopped finely

½ glass of white wine (optional)

50g/2oz goat's cheese

The flavour combinations in this are absolutely sensational. It's very simple and delicious and really worth trying out. As goat's cheese is not as cheap as, say, Cheddar, then maybe do it as a treat, but you could easily substitute Cheddar or even some blue cheese. Also, it's amazing where rosemary grows. At uni I found it growing in the back garden, so have a scout around your garden or your mates' gardens and you might find some growing near you.

1 Boil the water in a pan then crumble in your stock cubes. Reduce the heat to low and keep the stock simmering while you make the risotto.

2 In a saucepan, melt the butter over a low-medium heat

3 Reduce the heat t low and add the garl and the onion.

5 Increase the heat to medium-high and add the rice and the rosemary. Stir well so the rice soaks up the butter, onion and garlic. Next add the wine, if you're using it.

4 Cook for 5 minutes until the onion is soft.

6 Stir all the time to stop the rice sticking to the bottom of the pan. When each ladle of stock has been absorbed, add another. This process should take 15–20 minutes.

Keep tasting your risotto until it becomes deliciously creamy but still has a bit of bite to it.

7 When the wine has been absorbed by the rice, add a ladleful of stock and a pinch of salt.

8 Crumble in most of the cheese.

9 Season, stir and serve topped with the remaining cheese.

Optional Extras: Some chopped bacon bits would be delicious. A handful of rocket or watercress on top of the cooked risotto when you're ready to serve works well too. A drizzle of balsamic vinegar, if you have any, really brings out all the flavours – just add 1 teaspoon of this when you're ready to serve.

Serving Suggestions: This risotto is delicious if you mix in some pesto as well (see page 65). The risotto goes deliciously green and is known as a risotto verde.

Leftovers: Eat it all up, as this won't keep.

CAULIFLOWER CHEESE SERVES 1

This is great as a side veg with a roast or meaty dish, but don't underestimate how great it is just on its own as a speedy supper. While the cauliflower is cooking you can whip up a gorgeous, cheesy sauce and then brown it off under a grill or in the oven – perfect comfort food.

YOU WILL NEED:

½ head cauliflower, broken up into little florets

40g/1½ oz butter, plus extra for greasing

40g/1½ oz flour

200ml/7fl oz milk

350g/12oz Cheddar cheese, grated

Preheat the oven to 180°C/350°F/Gas Mark 4.

1 Boil a large pan of water and add the cauliflower. Boil for 6–7 minutes until the stalks are soft when pressed with a knife, then drain.

2 Meanwhile, gently melt the butter in a saucepan. Add the flou and stir well for 1–2 minutes.

3 Add the milk.

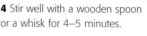

4 Stir well with a wooden spoon or a whisk for 4–5 minutes.

The lumps should start to dissolve and the milk will become thicker.

5 Stir in three-quarters of the cheese until it dissolves. Remove from the heat.

6 Grease the bottom of an ovenproof dish with butter and then scatter in the cauliflower.

The size I use is 20cm/8in long, 15cm/6in wide and 6cm/2½in deep, but it's not critical to use one exactly this size.

7 Pour over the cheese sauce, then scatter with the remaining grated cheese and bake in the oven for 10–15 minutes until bubbling and golden.

How good is that?

Heh heh!

Optional Extras: You could add some strips of ham over the cooked cauliflower florets before you add the cheese sauce – a delicious twist.

Serving Suggestions: This is great comfort food; serve with some boiled peas on the side for real home cooking.

Leftovers: Cheese sauce will keep in the fridge for up to 2 days. To reheat it simply pour it into a saucepan and heat up VERY slowly, stirring all the time. You could serve it this time with some pasta as a cheesy sauce and maybe with some bacon too. It's also very delicious over leeks – see gooey leek gratin (page 115) for a similar idea.

HOW TO MAKE A TOASTED SANDWICH

Toasted sandwiches are the best, most wonderful food when you've had a night out. Forget the calories, just add whatever you can find to make a gorgeous, fat, hot sandwich. My favourite ingredient in a toasty is cheese. I am assuming that you won't have a toasted sandwich maker. It might seem daft to write a recipe for a toasted sandwich, but I always want ideas for juicy mouth-watering fillings.

HAM AND CHEESE TOASTY SERVES 1

YOU WILL NEED:
2 slices of bread
1 teaspoon butter
1 teaspoon mayonnaise
3 slices of ham
3 slices of Cheddar cheese

1 Place the bread slices in your toaster and toast for 2 minutes until brown.

2 Remove from the toaster and spread with the butter and mayo.

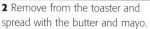
3 Add the slices of ham and cheese.

4 Then sandwich the bread slices together.

Easy peasy.

Optional Extras: You could add some lovely sliced tomatoes or even some lettuce leaves.
Serving Suggestions: Eat with a dollop of ketchup on the side.

BANANA TOASTY
SERVES 1

This might sound like a strange combination, but I used to adore banana toasties when I was a little girl, just adored them. I sometimes have them now and again, but it's got to be a great one after the pub. It hits both sweet and savoury cravings, killing two birds with one stone.

YOU WILL NEED:
2 slices of bread
1 banana
1 teaspoon butter
1 teaspoon sugar

3 Butter the toast and then pile the banana onto one slice.

1 Toast your bread.

2 Slice up the banana.

4 Sprinkle with the sugar and then sandwich them both together.

Optional Extras: You could add a teaspoon of chocolate spread here, which would be amazing. Brown sugar would work very well too.
Serving Suggestions: Eat with a lovely cuppa.

THE T CLUB SERVES 1

I regularly make this for friends, who've named it the T Club. In my eyes it's the king of the toasted sandwiches. Don't worry if you're missing some of the ingredients, just put in what you have or want.

1 Toast the bread. Meanwhile, get your ingredients ready.

2 Spread the toast with the butter, mayo and sweet chilli sauce.

4 Sandwich the whole lot together with the other slice of toast and carefully cut diagonally in half.

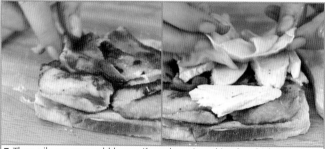

3 Then pile up your cold bacon if you have it and/or the chicken. Place your ham, cheese and avocado slices over the top.

5 Secure each half together using a cocktail stick.

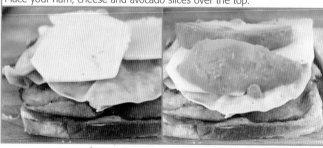

Optional Extras: Add or remove what you like. Lettuce Leaves are lovely in a toasty. Try adding ½ teaspoon of pesto (see page 65). You could also turn this into a wrap by placing all the ingredients in a tortilla.
Serving Suggestions: Eat with a load of napkins nearby, as you're guaranteed to spill.
Leftovers: Not worth keeping, so just eat it.

THE ULTIMATE CHEESE ON TOAST

SERVES 1

This is my stepmother's recipe for cheese on toast. It is utterly delicious and is in between cheese on toast and a welsh rarebit. The onion's flavour mellows under the grill but still manages to provide a little extra kick. It's classic comfort food.

Preheat the grill to high.

1 In a bowl, mix the onion, cheese, milk and Worcestershire sauce. Season well with salt and pepper.

Serve hot.

2 Spoon the mixture evenly over the bread slices.

3 Place under a hot grill.

4 Cook for 5–7 minutes until golden brown and bubbling.

Optional Extras: You could lay 2 slices of ham on each slice of bread before you spoon on the cheese mixture and then you have the ultimate ham and cheese on toast.

Serving Suggestions: Serve with a good squirt of ketchup and that's it.

HAM AND CHEESE OMELETTE
SERVES 1

YOU WILL NEED:
2 eggs
1 tablespoon milk
25g/1oz butter
1 teaspoon oil
2 tablespoons of grated Cheddar cheese
2 tablespoons of chopped ham

Omelettes are the *ultimate* fast food; they should be cooked in one minute and on a high heat. Follow these basic tips and your omelette should be perfect. Use a non-stick pan, preferably 10–12cm/8–9 inches in diameter. I use mainly butter and a drizzle of oil. This is because butter cooked on a very high heat burns but not once you add a little oil.

1 Crack the eggs into a bowl and add the milk. Use a whisk to mix just until the eggs and milk are combined, as you need to keep some air in the eggs to create a fluffy omelette. Add a good pinch of both salt and pepper.

2 Put your pan onto a high heat and add the butter and oil. When they are hot, after about 1 minute, add the egg mixture.

3 Using a spatula, start scraping the mixture from the outside of the pan into the middle. Tilt the pan to allow any un-cooked liquid egg to flow into the gaps and cook. It should take no more than a minute to cook. Don't forget the heat should be set to HIGH so you'll need to work quickly.

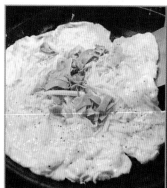

4 Scatter the cheese and ham over the middle of the omelette and shake the pan around a little. Carefully flip half of the omelette over the other half as this will make the cheese melt faster.

5 After a further 10 seconds, tip the folded omelette onto a plate and serve.

Optional Extras: As far as fillings are concerned you can really be as creative and have as much fun creating your favourite omelette as you want. They are great meals to use up leftovers like mushrooms, bacon, tomatoes, boiled potatoes or chicken. Add some chopped tomatoes for a delicious ham, cheese and tomato omelette.
Serving Suggestions: Eat with a green salad for a fresh feel.
Leftovers: This does not keep well or reheat well, but if you're only making one you should manage to eat it all.

SPANISH OMELETTE
SERVES 1

The Spanish call this a *tortilla* and serve it either hot or cold. It's ideal sliced up for picnics or a packed lunch. This is a good one for using up leftovers as well, and you can really put what you want in it. I make mine with potatoes, onions and tomatoes, but feel free to leave out or add ingredients depending on what you have.

1 Heat the oil in a 10–12cm/8–9 inch frying pan over a high heat. Add the potato slices and a good pinch of salt. Reduce the heat to medium and cook for about 5 minutes until golden. Remove the cooked potatoes from the pan and set aside.

> Don't worry about drawing the edges in as you would with a normal omelette, you want the edges to set.

2 Using the same pan, melt the butter over a medium heat, then tip in the beaten eggs.

3 Add the cooked potato slices, tomato and onion.

4 After about 3 minutes you should see the omelette begin to set. Next you need to turn the omelette onto the other side so it cooks evenly. To do this find a plate that's bigger than the pan you're using, turn the plate upside down (covering the pan) and turn the omelette onto the plate.

> **5** Slide the omelette back into the pan to cook the other side for 2 minutes. Serve.

Optional Extras: Be really experimental and add what you like. Bacon, peas, red onions, and pepperoni work well.
Serving Suggestions: Just as good cold and perfect to take to the library or uni as a snack. Cute as well with some drinks if you have mates coming round. You could cook it in the morning and serve it chopped up as snacks.
Leftovers: This will keep in the fridge for up to 2 days.

ONE POT CHICKEN THIGHS
SERVES 1

This is great when I get home tired and hungry. So quick and easy – you literally bung everything you want with your chicken into a roasting tray, pop it into the hot oven for 20 minutes and there you go. Easy and delicious. Don't forget you could always replace the chicken thighs with a piece of fish, if you want a change.

YOU WILL NEED:
- 1–2 chicken thighs
- 2 garlic cloves, peeled
- ½ red onion, peeled, halved and sliced
- 1 tomato, cut into wedges
- 2 tablespoons olive oil
- large sprig of rosemary
- basil leaves, to serve (optional)

Preheat the oven to 200°C/ 400°F/Gas Mark 6.

1 Put the chicken thighs, garlic, onion, and tomato in a roasting tray .

2 Drizzle with the olive oil and sprinkle with a pinch of salt.

Check that the chicken is cooked properly by cutting it open at the thickest point to make sure there is no sign of pink.

3 Add a sprig of rosemary and roast in the oven for 20 minutes until the chicken is cooked.

4 Tip onto a plate, add some basil, if you have it, and serve.

Optional Extras: Try roasting the chicken thighs with some new potatoes, lemon wedges, and thyme. A cheeky dash of white wine would make it even better.

Serving Suggestions: To make a heartier dish, serve with some mashed potato, chips or roast some baby new potatoes with the chicken.

Leftovers: Any leftover chicken will keep in the fridge for up to 2 days and can be used in a salad, pasta or risotto.

CHICKEN WRAPPED IN BACON
SERVES 1

YOU WILL NEED:
1 rasher of bacon, smoked or unsmoked
1 chicken breast
1 tablespoon olive oil

This is super speedy and very delicious, not to mention plain simple. The bacon smells amazing while it cooks, so you'll be guaranteed to be really hungry by the time it's ready to eat.

Preheat the oven to 180°C/350°F/Gas Mark 4.

2 Lay the bacon-wrapped chicken breast on a small roasting tray. Spoon the olive oil over the chicken.

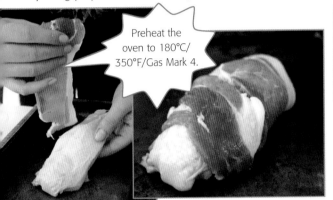

1 Simply wrap the bacon rasher around the chicken breast and tuck the ends underneath.

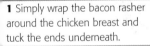

4 Remove from the oven after 20 minutes and serve hot.

3 Put in the oven for 15 minutes.

Optional Extras: I have left this very simple to prove how easy it can be. However, you could use garlic and crush it then rub it onto the chicken breast skin before you wrap it in the bacon. You might also want to take a sprig of rosemary or thyme and tuck it under the bacon for added flavour. Another delicious thing to do is take a slice of cheese (Cheddar would be fine, but another great option would be a little bit of blue cheese) just place a small slice of it under the bacon before you put it all in the oven.

Serving Suggestions: Serve with a drizzle of olive oil and some pasta, rice or a juicy tomato salad.

Leftovers: You can keep the cooked chicken in your fridge for 2 days. To reheat it, put it in an ovenproof dish, cover it with foil and warm it in an oven set to 110°C/225°F/Gas Mark ¼. It should take about 15 minutes to become piping hot. Served cold, it would be delicious sliced in a salad or with some couscous. You could even take it into uni for lunch.

3

FOOD
ON THE
MOVE

Every student becomes a master at being thrifty with their money. Days are spent hurrying from one lecture or tutorial to the next, and then before you know it, it's lunchtime. Regularly buying a salad or a sandwich and a drink can start to cost a fair bit, but if you make your own food to take into uni you can save your money for much better things instead.

I've included my favourite wraps, sandwiches, salads and couscous recipes here. They've served me well, being both delicious and portable. None of them take long to make, just give yourself 10 minutes extra in the morning and you'll be good to go.

TUNA AND SPRING ONION PITTA SERVES 1

Sandwiches are probably the most common item found in a lunchbox, and they are great. I love fiddling around with the fillings and even the breads. Normal bread is great, but rolls, wraps and pitta are also very delicious and it's good to keep changing your sandwich so you don't get bored. I always have wraps in my cupboard as they are healthy for lunch, and then in the evening transform into fajitas, another firm favourite.

YOU WILL NEED:
200g/7oz/1 can of tuna in brine
1 spring onion, chopped
1 tablespoon mayonnaise
1 tablespoon tomato ketchup
1 medium tomato, chopped
1–2 pitta breads
2–4 lettuce leaves

1 Drain the liquid out of your tin of tuna. Most tins of tuna are sold in brine, salt water or oil. I always get the one in brine as it's the healthiest and tastiest.

I was on holiday with a friend a few years ago, and when she made her picnic lunches for the beach she always put ketchup in her tuna sandwiches. I thought that was pretty odd at first but tried it and I have never looked back. Amazing...

2 Mix the tuna, spring onion, mayonnaise, ketchup and tomato. Taste and season with salt and pepper.

3 Toast your pitta.

Now tuck in.

4 Fill it with your tuna filling and then add a few lettuce leaves.

Optional Extras: Capers, chopped chives.
Serving Suggestions: You could fill your lunchbox with delicious treats such as crisps, a chocolate bar, and a mix of chopped carrots, cucumber and celery.
Leftovers: Any extra filling will keep in the fridge for 1–2 days and would be delicious in a jacket potato.

EGG MAYONNAISE SANDWICHES SERVES 1

Egg Mayonnaise reminds me of the delicious sandwiches on white bread I used to have in my lunchboxes when I was little. It's so simple but true tradition and a staple sandwich filler. Yum.

YOU WILL NEED:
2 medium eggs
1 tablespoon mayonnaise
1 teaspoon butter
2 slices of bread

1 Bring a pan of water to the boil. Lower the eggs, one by one, into the pan using a large spoon.

2 Cook for 8 minutes, then drain and refill the pan with cold water. Leave the eggs to cool for 2 minutes. When cool, gently knock the eggs on the side. Peel away and discard the shell.

3 I use a grater to grate the cooked eggs into a bowl, but you could also chop or slice the eggs or even mash them with a fork.

4 Stir the mayonnaise into the egg and add lots of salt and pepper.

5 Butter the bread and add the filling.

Optional Extras: Chopped chives, cress.
Serving Suggestion: I think this is great with good chunky hunky white bread.
Leftovers: The filling will keep in an airtight container in the fridge for 2 days.
Other Sandwich Filling Ideas: Ham and cheese, ham and mustard, chicken and sweetcorn, chicken and mayonnaise (also nice in jacket potatoes), ham and tomato, or classic cucumber.
It's great to beef sandwiches up with some lettuce, cucumber, mayonnaise and a bit of salt and pepper.

POTATO, BACON AND SPRING ONION SALAD
SERVES 1

This is simply gorgeous as a lunch and I love it with some chicken or just on its own for a nifty little supper.

3 Make sure the potatoes are cooked by pressing one with the tip of a sharp knife. It should be soft enough to go in easily.

1 Bring a pan of water to the boil and carefully add the potatoes. Boil for 10 minutes.

2 Meanwhile heat the oil in a frying pan and add the bacon. Fry on a medium heat for 4–5 minutes until crispy and golden. Tip onto kitchen towel to soak up some of the oil.

4 Drain the potatoes and tip them into a bowl. Add the crispy bacon and spring onions and mix in the mayonnaise.

Gorgeous!

Optional Extras: Little pieces of cooked chicken would be lovely thrown in at the end. Chopped coriander really adds to the flavours and I would recommend using a little if you wish. A lovely alternative to mayonnaise would be soured cream or crème fraîche.

Serving Suggestions: This works well with cold roast chicken, too (see pages 110–11). If you fancy a warm version, put the cooked potatoes in the same pan as the cooked bacon over a low heat, add the spring onions and replace the mayo with crème fraîche or soured cream. Add some chopped coriander and serve.

Leftovers: The cooked potatoes will keep on their own in the fridge for up to 4 days. Throw them into some simmering water for a couple of minutes just to take the chill out of them. The whole salad will go fairly soggy if kept for long in the fridge with the mayonnaise in it, so store the mayonnaise separately if you feel you won't need/eat it all.

CHICKPEA AND RED ONION SALAD SERVES 1

YOU WILL NEED:

200g/7oz canned chickpeas
½ red onion, chopped finely
½ long cucumber, cubed
1 garlic clove, peeled and
    chopped finely
juice of 1 lemon
1 tablespoon olive oil

Chickpeas are pale and shaped like hazelnuts. They are the staple ingredient in the delicious hummus dip, and chickpeas with lemon and olive oil are a great marriage. I always buy the ones canned in salted water, they are pre-cooked and don't involve any soaking or general messing around. They are abundantly available. This is a great on-the-go salad to take in for lunch and is über nutritious.

1 Mix all the ingredients together in a bowl and taste. The oil and chickpeas should be a great creamy taste.

2 Pack in an airtight container and there's your lunch.

Optional Extras: Try adding ¼ teaspoon ground cumin for a totally delicious variation, and scatter in some cold roast chicken (see pages 110–11). Chopped parsley would add a splash of colour, while crumbled feta would add an extra twist.
Serving Suggestions: Pack this with some pitta bread and it's a very filling lunch. This would be brilliant to serve in a big bowl for a house party, maybe with with some barbecue bits like the honey and mustard chicken (see page 137) or delicious juicy sausages (see page 136). Great with tsatsiki as well (see page 61).
Leftovers: This salad will keep in an airtight container in the fridge for up to 2 days.

CHICKEN AND TOMATO SALSA WRAP
MAKES 2 WRAPS

YOU WILL NEED:
1 teaspoon vegetable oil
1 chicken breast, sliced
1 garlic clove, peeled and
chopped finely
½ red pepper, deseeded and
chopped finely
1 medium tomato, chopped
½ teaspoon olive oil
pinch of sugar
2 plain tortilla wraps
handful of shredded lettuce
handful of grated Cheddar
cheese

In Newcastle there is a great deli, 'Dene's Deli', where a lot of the students go if they cannot be bothered to make lunch, and I have had the same wrap ever since I have been there. It's a whopper wrap with chicken, bacon, avocado, mozzarella, lettuce, mayonnaise and pesto. This wrap recipe, however, is a little simpler and inspired by a true student classic – the fajita!

1 Heat the oil in a frying pan, then add the chicken and garlic and lower the heat to medium.

2 Fry the chicken for 2 minutes, then add the peppers.

3 Cook for a further 3 minutes and check that your chicken is cooked by cutting it open with a knife to make sure there are no traces of pink flesh.

4 Mix the chopped tomato, olive oil and sugar together in a bowl.

5 Take a wrap and spoon the tomato salsa down the centre. Repeat with the other wrap.

6 Then add the chicken and red pepper mix.

8 Roll each wrap tightly around the filling.

7 Add the lettuce and grated Cheddar cheese.

Use some foil to hold the wraps together.

Optional Extras: Grated cheese, lettuce, soured cream, chillies.
Serving Suggestions: Wrap this in foil and take it into uni for lunch. Perfect. For more fajita ideas, see page 81.
Leftovers: Keep the cooked chicken mix covered in the fridge for up to 2 days. To reheat it, place it in the oven set to 110°C/225°F/Gas Mark ¼ for 15 minutes. The tomato salsa will keep in an airtight container in the fridge for 2 days.

HOW TO MAKE COUSCOUS

SERVES 1

YOU WILL NEED:

50g/2oz couscous

60ml/2½fl oz boiling water

Couscous is used extensively in Morocco and the Middle East and is often served with a meat or vegetable stew. It's brilliant eaten on its own, or as an accompaniment. Couscous is amazing with anything from chicken to roasted vegetables. It's perfect for lunch.

1 Put the couscous in a bowl

2 Pour over the boiling water.

3 Stir well and leave for 5 minutes.

The couscous will now have doubled in weight and more than doubled in size. It can be eaten hot or cold.

4 Mix around with a fork, fluffing it up so all the grains are loose and soft.

Optional Extras: Instead of using boiling water, add some flavour and replace the water with chicken or vegetable stock. You could add a teaspoon of olive oil or butter as well, to add a little flavour if you wish.

Serving Suggestions: Couscous is brilliant with meat such as casseroles and great if you have some spices lying around such as cumin or cardamom. It's good mixed into a salad, too.

Leftovers: Cooked couscous can be kept in a sealed container in your fridge for up to 3 days. To reheat it, put it in an ovenproof dish, sprinkle it with a little water and heat it slowly in an oven set to 110°C/225°F/Gas Mark ¼; however, it is perfectly good eaten cold.

COUSCOUS WITH RED ROASTED VEGETABLES SERVES 1

Absolutely delicious and nutritious as a salad, great if you're a vegetarian and perfect as a packed lunch. The sweetness of the tomatoes and red peppers makes this a true sensation.

YOU WILL NEED:

1 red pepper, deseeded and sliced
2 tomatoes, halved and quartered
½ red chilli, deseeded and chopped finely
2 garlic cloves, peeled and crushed
2 teaspoons olive oil
½ teaspoon sugar
50g/2oz couscous
60ml/2½fl oz boiling water

Preheat the oven to 200°C/400°F/ Gas Mark 6.

1 Place the red pepper, tomatoes, chilli and garlic in a roasting tray, drizzle with the olive oil and sprinkle with the sugar. This really enhances the sweetness in the tomatoes and peppers.

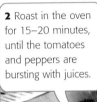

2 Roast in the oven for 15–20 minutes, until the tomatoes and peppers are bursting with juices.

3 Meanwhile cook the couscous by pouring over the boiling water, leaving it for 5 minutes and then fluffing it up (see opposite).

4 Add the juicy roasted veg to the couscous and either serve now or tip into a packed lunch box for later.

Optional Extras: There is so much you can do with this, and is one of my all-time favourite dishes. You could add all sorts of vegetables to the dish and roast them; red onions would work especially well quartered and roasted with the tomatoes and pepper. You could also crumble over some feta cheese, or mozzarella slices, although they can be slightly pricey. You could whip up some pesto, if you have some parsley or basil lying around (see page 65).

Serving Suggestions: A drizzle of balsamic vinegar works wonders with the flavours in this dish. Then tip it all into an airtight container for a perfectly portable packed lunch.

Leftovers: If you have leftovers and want to keep them for another day, I'd recommend storing both items in separate airtight containers in the fridge. If they are together the couscous will become really soggy and turn into a big mush. To reheat the veg, place them in an ovenproof dish and pop into the oven at 110°C/225°F/Gas Mark ¼ for 10 minutes.

MOROCCAN COUSCOUS SALAD SERVES 1

Often sold readymade in supermarkets, this is much more economical and tasty when you make it yourself. I love the combination of the couscous with raisins, cucumber, red onion, and yoghurt. It makes the thriftiest and tastiest of lunches.

YOU WILL NEED:
1 chicken or vegetable stock cube
60ml/2½fl oz boiling water
50g/2oz couscous
½ cucumber, diced
½ red onion, chopped finely
2 tablespoons mint, chopped
1 tablespoon raisins or currants
1 tablespoon olive oil
juice of 1 lemon

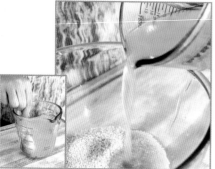

1 Mix the stock cube into the boiling water. Stir well until dissolved and then pour onto the couscous and leave to sit for 5 minutes.

2 Fluff up the couscous using a fork, then add the cucumber, red onion, mint and raisins or currants. Add the olive oil and lemon juice, mix well and season with some salt and pepper.

3 Mix well so that all the flavours are combined.

4 Pack your lunch in an airtight container and on your bike you go…

Optional Extras: A spice would be great here, and I would suggest ¼ teaspoon cumin to mix with the other ingredients. Chopped coriander or dried apricots would work well with the flavours here too.

Serving Suggestions: Obviously, these are all ideas of what to take for lunch into uni. However, don't think that you can't serve these up for dinner. Use some pitta bread as an edible scoop/spoon.

Leftovers: You can mix all the ingredients together and leave them tightly covered in the fridge for up to 2 days. This enables all the flavours to intensify and will leave you with a true taste of Morocco.

GREEN COUSCOUS SALAD SERVES 1

I love this as a really fresh and vibrant salad. Don't overcook the veg, as they're best with a bit of a crunch, and lots of lime juice. This is so tasty and nutritious to gobble up when you get a minute in your hectic day.

YOU WILL NEED:

75g/3oz frozen peas
50g/2oz fresh sugar snap peas
1 chicken or vegetable stock cube
60ml/2½fl oz boiling water
50g/2oz couscous
1 tablespoon olive oil
½ green chilli, deseeded and chopped finely
juice of 1 lime
50g/2oz feta cheese

1 Bring a medium saucepan of water to the boil, and add the peas and sugar snap peas. Cook uncovered for 3–4 minutes.

2 Meanwhile mix the stock cube into the boiling water and pour over the couscous. Leave to stand for 5 minutes, then fluff it up with a fork.

3 Drain the peas and sugar snaps, and add them to the couscous.

5 Mix it all up and have a taste. It should be fresh and vibrant. Tip it into an airtight container.

4 Add the olive oil, green chilli and lime juice.

6 Crumble over the feta and serve.

Optional Extras: Anything green… Try herbs such as coriander, parsley or basil. Some green peppers or a drizzle of pesto would be tasty. What about frozen broad beans or even fresh ones? You could replace the feta with goat's cheese.
Serving Suggestions: For lunch I have it just as it is. However, this would be delicious with some roast chicken and is great with a summer barbecue. It tastes best chilled, so put an ice pack in your bag if it's going to be your packed lunch.
Leftovers: If you plan to keep this for longer than a morning, keep the couscous separate from the vegetables. Keep them in airtight containers in the fridge for up to 2 days.

4

HEALTHY DAYS FOR THE GIRLS

So, girls, what do we like? For sure the same stuff as the boys now and again, but salads and soups are great for lunch too. I've included some recipes here that are ideal for a girls' night in. A great big stir-fry is always popular. Get everyone to help you with the chopping and throw in some rice or noodles to fill everyone up. Alternatively you could have a sort of indoor picnic – I love it when my girlfriends come round and sit on the floor tucking into crudités, tsatsiki and bruschetta while we gossip. Food like this requires very little cooking and lends the evening a relaxed feel. Easy food for nights when you're all going to sit in front of a film or just chill with a bottle of wine for a good catch-up chat.

CAESAR SALAD

SERVES 2–4

This is a true tradition in our home. Leftover chicken and bacon seem so lonely and unappealing in the fridge, but they're given new life in this salad. If you can, try to make the dressing too – it's a real winner.

1 Heat the olive oil in a frying pan then add the bacon. Fry for 4 minutes until golden brown. Drain the lardons and set aside.

2 Put the lettuce on a plate and sprinkle over the cheese and bacon.

4 This is the part where you have to be quite careful. DON'T add all the oil at once. Add it bit by bit or it will curdle. Take your time. By the end your dressing should be creamy and smooth.

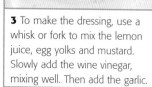

3 To make the dressing, use a whisk or fork to mix the lemon juice, egg yolks and mustard. Slowly add the wine vinegar, mixing well. Then add the garlic.

5 Season with salt and pepper, pour the dressing over the salad and serve.

Optional Extras: Chicken is often used in a Caesar salad, although traditionally it is made without. Don't let this hold you back, however. Feel free to add strips of cooked chicken if you wish. Olives and anchovies would also be delicious.
Serving Suggestions: You could serve this in a big salad bowl and let everyone help themselves.
Leftovers: Keep any bacon or chicken leftovers from anything else for this salad. However, a dressed salad will not keep so if you think your mates won't eat it all, add the dressing to each portion as needed. You could then cover the remaining lettuce leaves, bacon and cheese and keep them in the fridge for up to 2 days.

CRUDITÉ SELECTION WITH TSATSIKI
SERVES 2–4

In French *crudité* means raw. I serve these when I don't fancy cooking and have some friends coming round. It's a Mediterranean feast and always goes down well. A great alternative to the usual crisps and dips.

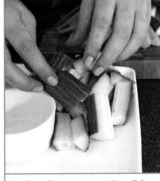

1 Chop all the vegetables and toast the pitta.

2 Place them on a serving dish.

3 In a small bowl, mix the yoghurt, cucumber, olive oil and lemon juice.

Optional Extras: Radishes are delicious, as are chicory and raw broccoli, which are eaten a lot in France. Half a teaspoon of ground cumin would be amazing in the tsatsiki.

Serving Suggestions: They look so beautiful all on a big serving plate or even in a basket if you have one. You could make more of the tsatsiki and put it in a big bowl in the middle so everyone can have a dip.

Leftovers: The raw vegetables will keep for 2 days in the fridge, tightly covered, as will the tsatsiki.

WARM SALAD NIÇOISE
SERVES 2–4

This is a wonderful tasty dish. I love the warmth of the ingredients combined with the crisp crunch of the lettuce leaves. If you are on a bigger budget you might use a tuna steak instead of canned tuna.

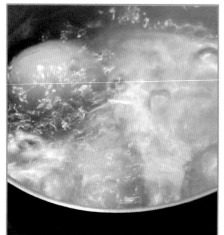

1 Place the eggs in a saucepan of boiling water and cook for 8 minutes.

2 Place the potatoes in a pan of water. Bring to the boil, cook for 5 minutes, then add the beans and cook for a further 5 minutes.

4 Drain the potatoes and beans. Scatter the beans over the lettuce.

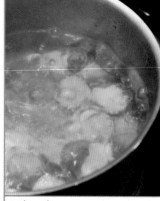

3 Meanwhile, put the lettuce leaves in some serving bowls, and sprinkle them with the spring onions.

5 Scatter the tuna onto the salad.

6 Then add the cooked potatoes.

7 Drain the eggs and put them in cold water for 2 minutes to cool. Peel away the shells, then cut the eggs in half and add them to the salad.

8 Carefully arrange the olives or anchovies, if you're using them, over the tuna.

9 Mix the dressing ingredients together and pour over the salad. Add salt and pepper and serve.

Serving Suggestions: Serve with a good hunk of warm bread.

Leftovers: If the salad has been dressed it doesn't keep well at all and wilts very badly. Therefore if it looks like you will have leftovers, get everyone to add their own dressing and then cover the remaining salad tightly and put it in the fridge to eat the next day.

Optional Extras: Olives and anchovies work very well here with the tuna. However, you could add whatever you like, such as tomatoes or cucumber. It's a salad, so just chuck in the things you like.

BRUSCHETTA

SERVES 2–4

In Italy, bruschetta is also called *fettunata* and this means, oiled slice. It's absolutely one of my favourite things in the world, I am such a fan of garlic and all things Italian, so this for me is true heaven, student or not! It's perfect for when you have some friends round and everyone can tuck in, or you could even have it for a lunch or dinner on your own.

YOU WILL NEED:

4 slices of bread – I use ciabatta

5 garlic cloves, peeled

4 tablespoons olive oil

4 tomatoes, halved, seeds removed and flesh chopped

2 tablespoons chopped basil

Preheat the grill.

1 Cut 2 of the garlic cloves in half and rub the cut side of the garlic over the slices of bread. Drizzle with half the olive oil.

2 Place the bread under the grill to brown for 3 minutes, then turn and continue grilling for a further 3 minutes.

4 Remove the bread from the grill and top with the tomato mixture. Eat immediately.

3 Meanwhile finely chop the remaining garlic and mix it with the tomatoes and basil. Pour over the remaining olive oil. Taste and season with salt and pepper, if needed.

Optional Extras: Where to start? There is so much you can add to this but it obviously depends on your budget. I love to add avocado slices, mozzarella, and a little pesto to it.

Serving Suggestions: It's so delicious as it is, so just tuck in.

Leftovers: The filling will keep on its own, covered and in the fridge, for up to 2 days. However, don't leave the actual bruschetta in the fridge as the bread will go extremely soggy.

HOMEMADE PESTO
SERVES 4

YOU WILL NEED:

4 tablespoons finely chopped parsley
2 garlic cloves, peeled and crushed
1 tablespoon grated Parmesan cheese
1 tablespoon finely chopped pinenuts (optional)
juice of ½ lemon
4 tablespoons olive oil

This is not officially the world's most common student dish; however, at uni I am always asked how to make pesto, and I can totally understand why. It's delicious, and a batch will keep in the fridge for 4–5 days, during which time you can use it on anything from pasta to pizza to bruschetta. It's up to you which herbs to use; I love basil pesto the most, but parsley pesto is very common too.

1 Mix together the parsley, garlic, Parmesan cheese, pinenuts and lemon juice.

3 Taste and season with salt and pepper. If you want it thicker, add some more herbs, or more olive oil if you want it thinner.

2 Then mix in the olive oil.

Optional Extras: This is a list of traditional ingredients for pesto, but if you want to cut costs, leave out the pinenuts.
Serving Suggestions: This is perfect spooned over the top of a bruschetta (see opposite). It's great with pasta as a very easy sauce, and also so delicious with chicken, and on pizzas. Try it added to a T Club Sandwich (see page 40).
Leftovers: Keep it tightly covered in the fridge for 4–5 days. When you use it again make sure you stir it well.

LOW CALORIE VEGETABLE SOUP SERVES 4

This is my staple lunch if I am watching my weight. I say this, but it tastes great and would be wrong to put it in the same category as dreadful 'diet food'. I don't liquidise it, I just put everything into one big pan, and love it über chunky. Perfect as a winter warmer.

YOU WILL NEED:
2 vegetable stock cubes
1 litre/1¾ pints boiling water
1 red chilli, deseeded and chopped roughly
2 garlic cloves, peeled and crushed
2 carrots, peeled and sliced
2 leeks, sliced
1 parsnip, peeled and chopped finely
½ head of broccoli, cut into florets
800g/2lb canned chopped tomatoes
1 sprig rosemary

1 In a pan, stir the stock cubes into the boiling water. Add all the chopped ingredients.

2 Add the tomatoes.

3 Add the rosemary sprig, hot stock and season with salt and pepper.

4 Put on a medium heat and boil for about 30 minutes, until all the vegetables are tender.

5 You can either liquidise it with a hand held blender or serve it as a really chunky soup with a good hunk of bread.

6 Grind some more pepper over the top and serve.

Optional Extras: Add any vegetables you fancy; herbs such as basil or parsley are great in this too.
Serving Suggestions: I love this with lots of pepper ground over the top, and that's it.
Leftovers: I find there are leftovers of most soups, but you can keep this in the fridge, covered, for up to 3 days. When you want to eat it, bring it briefly to the boil and serve.

TIFF'S HEALTHY MINESTRONE SOUP

SERVES 2–4

I adore minestrone soup, possibly because I'm a fan of chunky soups and this is the king of chunky. The pasta makes it very hearty while the tomatoes add a crucial sweetness. Make a big bowl and let everyone help themselves; for added pleasure, grate some cheese on top.

1 Heat the olive oil in a deep frying pan. Fry the bacon, onion and garlic for 4–5 minutes until the bacon is starting to brown.

3 Add the carrots, tomatoes and stock to the frying pan.

2 Meanwhile, stir the stock cubes into the boiling water.

4 Bring the soup to the boil, then reduce the heat and simmer over a medium heat for 15 minutes until all the vegetables are soft. Season with salt and pepper.

5 Add the pasta and cook for a further 10 minutes until the pasta is cooked.

Serve immediately.

Optional Extras: Chopped rosemary would work brilliantly in this, as would a glass of red wine.
Serving Suggestions: Eat with some bread and grate some cheese over the soup.
Leftovers: The soup will keep in the fridge for up to 3 days. Before eating it again, bring the soup briefly to the boil and serve piping hot.

HOW TO COOK NOODLES SERVES 2–4

Noodles are absolutely brilliant with all sorts of oriental style meals. It's easy to do a big curry or stir-fry and then have some gorgeous noodles to eat it with. They are brilliant in salads and soups, too. Cooking noodles really depends on which type you choose. Rice noodles are perfect just left in a bowl and covered with boiling water; egg noodles need to be boiled. Hardly rocket science, however.

EGG NOODLES

YOU WILL NEED:
350g/12oz egg noodles

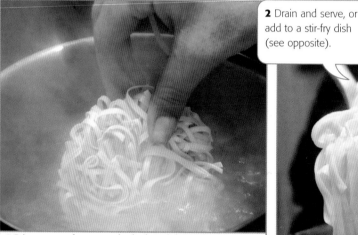

1 Bring a pan of water to the boil, and then add the egg noodles. Cook for 4 minutes.

2 Drain and serve, or add to a stir-fry dish (see opposite).

RICE NOODLES

YOU WILL NEED:
225g/8oz rice noodles

1 Place the noodles in a bowl and cover them with boiling water.

2 Leave to stand for 5 minutes until soft, then drain and serve, or add to a stir-fry dish (see opposite).

BEEF NOODLE STIR-FRY
SERVES 2–4

you go to a Chinese restaurant you'll doubtless find a selection of chow
hein dishes on the menu. It is the generic term used for a Chinese dish
f stir-fried noodles. You could use chicken, vegetables or even small
rawns instead of the beef in this recipe.

YOU WILL NEED:

225g/8oz rice noodles or
   egg noodles
2 tablespoons olive oil
2 red chillies, deseeded and
   chopped
2 tablespoons chopped ginger
2 garlic cloves, crushed
1 green pepper, deseeded and
   chopped finely
3 sirloin or rump steaks, sliced
juice of 2 limes
3 tablespoons soy sauce
1 teaspoon honey

Cook the rice
noodles
(see opposite).

2 Meanwhile, heat the oil in a
frying pan, then add the chillies,
ginger, garlic and green pepper.
Stir-fry for 4 minutes.

3 Add the beef, lime juice and soy sauce.
Fry for a couple of minutes.

4 Add the
cooked rice
noodles.

5 Mix well and add the honey. Have a taste
and add some more soy sauce if you think
it needs it.

Optional Extras: Teriyaki sauce instead of the soy sauce is truly delicious and you could use more vegetables if you want.
Serving Suggestions: Serve in a big bowl with a wedge of lime and tuck in with some chopsticks.
Leftovers: This stir-fry will keep in the fridge, covered, for up to 2 days. When you want to reheat it, blast it in a wok or
frying pan until it's piping hot.

PRAWN AND COCONUT STIR-FRY

SERVES 2–4

YOU WILL NEED:
2 tablespoons olive oil
1cm/½ inch piece of ginger,
   peeled and chopped finely
3 garlic cloves, peeled and
   crushed
3 spring onions, chopped
1 green chilli, chopped
4 tablespoons coconut milk
285g/11oz small ready-cooked
   prawns
1 tablespoon chopped
   coriander

I love a good pungent stir-fry – great when you have some mates round. It's easy to find ready-cooked prawns at the supermarket, so all you have to do is add them at the end. Add a few noodles and you're done.

1 Heat the oil in a frying pan, then add the ginger, garlic, spring onions and chilli.

2 Fry for 2 minutes, stirring constantly. You should be hit with delicious and fragrant flavours.

4 Right at the end throw in your prawns.

3 Add the coconut milk and mix around for 3 minutes until hot.

Optional Extras: I sometimes like to add some chopped cashew nuts or peanuts to this.
Serving Suggestions: Eat with delicious coconut noodles (see opposite).
Leftovers: Unfortunately this doesn't keep well because of the prawns. So eat up!

5 Scatter with coriander and serve.

COCONUT NOODLES

SERVES 2–4

YOU WILL NEED:
850ml/1½ pints coconut milk
350g/12oz egg noodles

love this method of cooking noodles. By cooking them in coconut milk, they gain a brilliant fragrant taste.

1 Pour the coconut milk into a saucepan and bring to the boil.

2 Add the noodles and cook for 4 minutes. Turn the heat off and leave them in the pan to infuse for 5 minutes.

Optional Extras: You could add some sliced ginger to make the flavour stronger and more intense.
Serving Suggestions: I would serve the coconut noodles with a prawn and coconut stir-fry (see opposite).
Leftovers: You could keep the coconut milk used for boiling the noodles for when you make a curry or stir-fry. It will keep, covered, in the fridge for 2 days.

5

BOYS ARE BACK IN TOWN

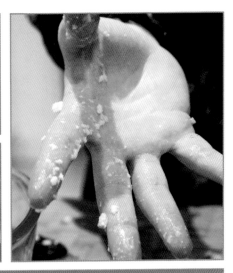

This might just be my favourite chapter. I love the student classic: a Mexican feast with tacos and fajitas. It's fun and perfect for a Friday night and it goes without saying that it's definitely not exclusively for boys. Get some tequila shots in and your Friday night will be better than ever. Then for the hangover the next day, there are delicious homemade burgers that you can pile high with cheese and salad. The minute steak sandwich is a boys' Saturday lunch favourite in front of the footie, whilst the hot hot curry will test you all to see how much spice you can handle. Last but not least you'll find classics like good old sausage and mash, and wonderful ways to cook and serve comforting jacket potatoes. Get stuck in!

HOW TO BAKE A JACKET POTATO

SERVES 2

A jacket potato is a wonderful supper and you can be as adventurous as you like with your filling. Personally, I love ham and cheese – you spoon out the inside, mix it with the cheese and ham, spoon it all back in and stick it under the grill to brown. It's comfort food at its best. A jacket potato might seem very basic; however, when we first moved into our house I was asked by a housemate – no names mentioned – how to cook one, so here's how!

2 Rub the oil over both potatoes and rub in some salt.

1 Preheat the oven to 200°C/400°F/Gas Mark 6. Prick the skin 3–4 times.

3 Bake in the oven for an hour, until crispy. To test if the potatoes are cooked, run a skewer or fork into a potato – it should be lovely and soft.

Optional Extras: If you fancy a less crispy skin, wrap the potatoes in foil. That way they will have a very soft inside and not such a crispy outside. I, however, am a massive fan of the crispy skin.

Leftovers: Cooked jacket potatoes can be kept in the fridge for 3 days. To reheat, simply heat the oven to 150°C/300°F/Gas Mark 2 and warm them through for 15 minutes.

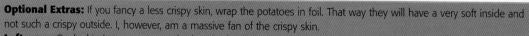

HAM AND CHEESE IN THEIR JACKETS

SERVES 4

love this and I find it such a great way of using up leftover ham and cheese. You create a really delicious filling by spooning out the potato inside mixing with all sorts, then spooning it all back in. When your work is getting you down, make yourself a jacket potato and I am sure all will seem much better.

1 Preheat the oven to 200°C/400°F/Gas Mark 6. Bake the potatoes as described opposite. Set aside for 5 minutes to cool.

2 Cut the potatoes in half and gently scoop out the hot potato inside, leaving the skins intact. Put the inside in a large mixing bowl.

3 Mix the butter, ham and cheese with the potato, and season with salt and pepper. It should be quite creamy and very delicious.

4 Spoon the filling back into the potato skins and top with more cheese.

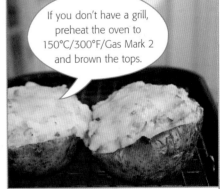

If you don't have a grill, preheat the oven to 150°C/300°F/Gas Mark 2 and brown the tops.

5 Place under a hot grill for 3–4 minutes until the cheese is golden.

Optional Extras: A couple of crushed garlic cloves would be brilliant added to the ham and cheese, as would some chopped herbs – I would suggest 2 tablespoons of chopped rosemary.
Serving Suggestions: Eat with a crisp green salad on the side.
Leftovers: Any leftovers will keep in the fridge for 3 days. To reheat, place in the oven at 150°C/300°F/Gas Mark 2 for 15 minutes until hot.

THE CLASSIC – JACKET POTATO WITH BEANS AND CHEESE SERVES 4

YOU WILL NEED:
4 large white potatoes
2 tablespoons vegetable oil
900g/2lb baked beans
  (2 cans)
110g/4oz butter
200g/7oz Cheddar cheese,
  grated

This is such a delicious way to gobble up a jacket potato. Warm beans and gorgeously gloopy melting cheese – for me it's food heaven!

1 Preheat the oven to 200°C/400°F/ Gas Mark 6. Bake the potatoes (see page 74).

2 Meanwhile empty the beans into a saucepan and heat on high, stirring all the time until hot. This should take about 5 minutes.

3 Cut the potatoes in half and add the butter.

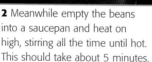

4 Spoon over the beans and scatter with grated cheese. Eat immediately.

Optional Extras: I don't think that this delicious meal needs anything else. However, my friend Bex thoroughly recommends cottage cheese as a healthy alternative to Cheddar. Use 1–2 tablespoons of cottage cheese per jacket potato.
Serving Suggestions: Gobble up on a plate with a good beer.
Leftovers: Beans can be kept in the fridge, covered with clingfilm, for 3–4 days. To reheat cook on medium-high, stirring, for about 5 minutes till hot. NEVER leave cans open in the fridge, always tip the contents into a bowl and cover.

SATURDAY MINUTE STEAK SANDWICH

SERVES 2–4

The footie is on, boys, and the beers are flowing. So what do you need now? A steak sandwich oozing with mustard and ketchup. Toss a coin to see which one of you will rack up the sandwiches, or even better all get involved and try and get it done before kick-off.

YOU WILL NEED:

4 ciabatta rolls
2 tablespoons olive oil
2 garlic cloves, halved
1 tablespoon vegetable oil
4 beef frying steaks
4 teaspoons mustard
4 tomatoes, sliced
100g/3½oz lettuce leaves, rocket leaves work wonders here

Turn on the grill to high; if you don't have one set the oven to 50°C/300°F/Gas Mark 2.

1 Slice open the rolls, drizzle them with olive oil and rub with the cut side of the garlic cloves.

2 Set under the grill to crisp up for 5–6 minutes, turning half way through. Remove and set aside.

3 Heat the vegetable oil in a frying pan, add the steaks, and cook on a high heat for 1–2 minutes on each side. Remove from the pan and leave to rest. They should still be pink in the middle.

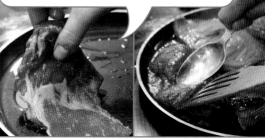

5 Add the lettuce leaves, close up the rolls and eat immediately.

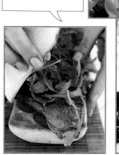

4 Spoon 1 teaspoon of mustard over each roll. Add the tomato slices and then the cooked steaks. Slice the steaks if you wish.

Optional Extras: It's your sandwich so feel free to add ketchup, or to take out the mustard. This is just my take on a steak sandwich but I am very aware that it's a personal thing.
Serving Suggestions: Devour with some chips and a beer.
Leftovers: I don't advise any leftover suggestions as you will have to eat it all – especially if you're boys. Eat up!

MEXICAN FEAST SERVES 2–4

This is the best, most brilliantly fun meal to whip up and eat on a Friday night with some mates before you go out. Delicious fajitas, guacamole and tacos and maybe a few Mexican drinking games. Watch out, because as soon as your sombreros are on, someone will whip out the tequila and then you've had it. You might not make it to the pub or club. Mexican food consists of fajitas, nachos, quesadillas, guacamole and lots more. You can buy brilliant kits in supermarkets now that are very reasonable, but if you make your own you'll probably get more for less money, and of course it'll taste better too.

GUACAMOLE

YOU WILL NEED:
2 ripe avocados, peeled, stones removed and sliced
1 red chilli, deseeded and chopped finely
3 garlic cloves, peeled and crushed
juice of 1 lime
5 tablespoons olive oil

1 Mix all the ingredients together in a bowl.

Serving Suggestions: This is brilliant with a Mexican feast to accompany fajitas and nachos. However, it's also amazing on a burger (see pages 84–85), or with crudités (see page 61) and crisps. It's brilliantly versatile.
Leftovers: Avocados react with oxygen in the air and go brown very quickly, so if you make this try and use it very quickly or press clingfilm right onto the surface of the guacamole so there are no air bubbles. You can keep it in the fridge for up to an hour, but no longer.

2 Mash the avocados using a fork or masher. Season very well with salt and pepper.

MEXICAN SPICY TOMATO SALSA

1 Place all the ingredients in a bowl and mix together well. Taste, and season with salt and pepper.

HOT TACOS SERVES 2-4

amazing, and a real must whenever you're going all Mexican. Taco trays or tortilla crisps are so easy to buy. Just add some toppings and away you go.

Preheat the oven to 180°C/350°F/ Gas Mark 4.

1 Put the taco trays on a baking sheet. Spoon in the salsa, soured cream and guacamole. Sprinkle with the cheese.

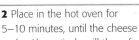

2 Place in the hot oven for 5–10 minutes, until the cheese melts. Alternatively grill them for 5 minutes.

QUESADILLAS

SERVES 2–4

These are what the Mexicans eat as a sandwich, and I'm a mega fan.
In Spanish the word translates exactly as 'little cheese thing', and the
cheese is what makes it so good. You use the same tortillas as you would
use for a fajita, so keep some aside if you're making these too. You can
cut quesadillas into cute bite-size triangles for party snacks, too.

YOU WILL NEED:
4 flour tortillas
4 tablespoons Guacamole
  (see page 78)
4 tablespoons soured cream
4 tablespoons Mexican Spicy
  Tomato Salsa (see page 79)
250g/9oz Cheddar cheese,
  grated

1 Take 1 tortilla and spread it with half the guacamole, soured cream and salsa, then sprinkle with half the cheese.

Repeat with the second quesadilla.

2 Take another tortilla and sandwich it on top of the one with all the filling. Repeat this with the remaining two tortillas. You will now have two pancake sandwiches or quesadillas.

3 Heat a frying pan over a low heat. Warm one quesadilla in the pan for 3–4 minutes until brown on one side. Turn it over to brown the other side.

4 Cut each quesadilla into triangles and serve hot.

Incredible.

Optional Extras: You could spice it up by adding some chillies or jalapeños. You could also add some cooked chicken or beef pieces, although I prefer to save the meat for Fajitas (see opposite).
Serving Suggestions: Eat as part of a Mexican meal with tacos and fajitas. If you just want a few light bites then these are great with drinks before you go out, or when you have some mates round and don't want to cook a big meal.
Leftovers: Quesadillas will go soggy in the fridge, so try to eat them all up.

FAJITAS SERVES 2-4

This is basically a Mexican wrap made with beef, lots of sauces and some cheese. Serve them hot with some delicious Mexican beer and your evening will be made!

1 Heat the oil in a frying pan, then add the garlic and the steak. Cook over a high heat for 3–4 minutes. When ready it should still be slightly pink in the middle.

YOU WILL NEED:

- 1 tablespoon vegetable oil
- 2 garlic cloves, peeled and crushed
- 4 thin frying steaks, sliced
- 4 flour tortillas
- 4 tablespoons Mexican Spicy Tomato Salsa (see page 79)
- 4 tablespoons soured cream
- 4 tablespoons Guacamole (see page 78)
- 4 handfuls shredded iceberg lettuce
- 250g/9oz Cheddar cheese, grated

2 Remove from the heat and set aside to rest. Meanwhile assemble your fajitas.

4 Roll up the wrap, and repeat to make three more fajitas. Brilliant.

3 Take one tortilla and spoon over 1 tablespoon of salsa, followed by the same amount of soured cream and guacamole. Add a few steak slices, then sprinkle with a handful of lettuce and some grated cheese.

Optional Extras: Try this with pan-fried chicken instead of steak. You could add some sliced, deseeded chillies to it too, for a hotter version.

Serving Suggestions: Serve this with a selection of other Mexican dishes, such as Hot Tacos (see page 79) and Quesadillas (see opposite). Wash it down with some Mexican beer, sombreros on your heads and maybe even some Tequila shots to finish.

Leftovers: Not great, so just get eating.

SAUSAGE AND MASH UP
SERVES 2–4

When I first began uni, 'mash up' was the term used to describe partying and mashed potato. A weird combination; however, mash was very often consumed on a Friday night before going out partying and eaten with lots of mates, beer and wine. You can add just milk, cream and seasoning to it, but you could also add mustard, pesto, garlic, peas, apricots, rosemary, or cheese. It's so versatile, just remember to season well.

YOU WILL NEED:

10 large white potatoes, such as Maris Pipers, chopped roughly

1 tablespoon vegetable oil

8 sausages

100g/3½ oz butter

150ml/5fl oz double cream

15ml/5fl oz milk

1 Put the potatoes in a large saucepan of water and bring to the boil for about 15 minutes.

2 Meanwhile heat the oil in a frying pan and add the sausages. Cook on a medium heat for 10–15 minutes until golden brown.

3 Drain the potatoes then put them back in the pan. Mash them until there are no lumps and then add the butter. Mix well and mash in the cream and milk.

4 Taste, and season very well with salt and pepper. Serve with the cooked sausages.

Serving Suggestions: A plate piled high with mash, sausages and a good squeeze of ketchup and mustard.
Leftovers: Cold cooked sausages will keep in the fridge for 3 days and are fab eaten cold. To reheat them, place them in a frying pan over a medium heat for 5 minutes.

MASHED POTATO VARIATIONS

SERVES 2–4

As I mention above, the additions to mashed potato are endless. Here are a few of my favourites.

Mustard Mash
Using the recipe opposite, add 3 tablespoons of English mustard with the milk and cream.

Pea Mash
This is an Irish recipe and is wonderful as an accompaniment or just eaten on its own.

1 Bring a small pan of water to the boil and add 300g/12oz frozen peas. Cook for 5 minutes. Drain and add the peas to the mash along with the cream and milk.

Pesto Mash
Add 3 tablespoons pesto (see page 65) with the butter and do not add the cream or milk.

Cheesy Mash
Add 110g/4oz grated cheese with the milk and cream.

Garlic Mash
Add 3 crushed garlic cloves to the mash along with the milk and cream.

Optional Extras: Add 2 tablespoons finely chopped rosemary and/or 2 peeled, crushed garlic cloves to the plain mash along with the milk and cream.

HOMEMADE BEEF BURGERS WITH RUSTIC CHIPS

MAKES 4 BURGERS

Preheat the oven to 200°C/400°F/Gas Mark 6.

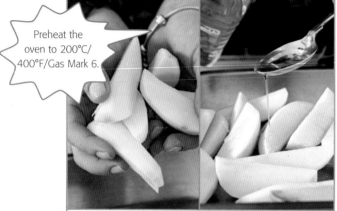

1 Cut the potatoes into wedges; you should get 4–6 wedges from each potato. Place them on a baking tray, drizzle with half the olive oil and season with salt.

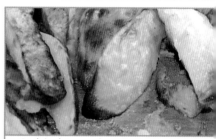

2 Cook in the oven for 20–30 minutes until golden brown and soft.

3 Meanwhile mix the mince with the onion, garlic, chilli, parsley and 1 tablespoon olive oil. Use your hands to divide the mixture into 4, then shape into burgers about 2.5cm/1 inch thick.

4 Heat the remaining oil in a frying pan and add the burgers. Cook on a medium heat for 5 minutes. Turn and cook for a further 5 minutes. The burgers should be brown on the outside and cooked through, with hardly any trace of pink inside. After 10–12 minutes they should be ready.

5 Add 2 slices of cheese to the top of each burger, just before they're ready.

6 Assemble the burgers by sandwiching a few lettuce leaves, a burger, a tomato slice and a squirt of ketchup and mayonnaise in each bun.

Serve with the hot chips – yum!

Optional Extras: Place a cube of cheese – I like Cheddar, or even blue cheese – inside the mince mixture. Do this once you have shaped them into burgers and before you cook them. Then when you take a bite you'll get melted cheese inside your cooked burger – amazing. Or place a slice of cheese on each burger 2 minutes before they are ready and watch it melt over your delicious burgers. In the summer, sundried tomatoes are gorgeous added to the mixture.

Serving Suggestions: I love to have my burger in a bun with ketchup, cheese on top, lettuce, tomato and a spot of mayo. Guacamole (see page 78) is also gorgeous, as are fried bacon and some fried onions. Up to you entirely.

Leftovers: Leave the raw mixture in the fridge for up to a day and then shape and cook. If you have some leftover raw mixture and you don't want to make another burger, form it into little balls to make your own meatballs. Cook in a pan and serve with spaghetti and tomato and garlic sauce (see page 27).

HOT HOT LAMB CURRY SERVES 4

How brave are you? This curry is punchy and spicy, perfect for a lads' night in with a few beers. It is very spicy, so if you want to tone it down leave out the chilli flakes and use a couple of fresh green chillies instead.

YOU WILL NEED:

- 1kg/2¼ lb lamb, diced
- 4 tablespoons plain yoghurt, plus extra to serve
- 1 teaspoon ground turmeric
- 1 teaspoon ground cumin
- 2 tablespoons vegetable oil
- 1 onion, peeled and sliced
- 3 garlic cloves, peeled and chopped finely
- 2cm/1inch piece of root ginger, peeled and chopped finely
- 6 small green chillies, such as bird's eye chillies
- 1–2 teaspoons chilli flakes
- 400ml/14fl oz boiling water
- 2 chicken stock cubes
- large handful of spinach leaves
- 4 tablespoons coriander leaves, chopped

1 Mix the lamb, yogurt, turmeric and cumin together in a bowl. Put in the fridge for an hour to marinate.

2 Heat the oil in a large pan and fry the onion, garlic and ginger.

3 Add the chillies and chilli flakes and mix around.

5 Mix up the boiling water and stock cubes, then pour over the lamb. Cook over a low heat for 35 minutes until the lamb is tender.

4 Add the yoghurt-marinated lamb, stir well and season with salt and pepper.

6 Add the spinach and cook for another 5 minutes.

7 Serve hot, hot, hot with a dollop of yoghurt to cool the flames!

Optional Extras: Feel free to use coconut milk instead of stock here. Red chillies would also be great and give the dish some extra colour.

Serving Suggestions: Serve with some buttered basmati rice with coriander (see page 125), some naan bread and a good mango chutney.

Leftovers: You can reheat the curry the following day by slowly bringing it to the boil in a pan set over a low heat. Alternatively, it can be frozen for up to 2 months.

6

TIFF'S TUESDAYS

What are Tiff's Tuesdays? They began in my second year at university after I had a few people round for supper one Tuesday. My friends asked if this could happen weekly; they came round on a Tuesday and I cooked. I was delighted; however, like all students with an eye on my bank balance, I suggested that they each chip in a fiver for the meal. They all agreed and it was deal done – Tiff's Tuesdays were born.

This chapter has some recipes to help you prepare your own thrifty mid-week feast. Don't feel rude asking people to chip in – it's all part of it. It's good food that will make your Tuesdays seem better than they have ever been.

HOW TO COOK PIZZA

One Tuesday at uni my friends all called me up and said they were broke due to it being end of term. I quietly checked my cupboards and explored what I had after a term of buying all sorts of bits. I found a can of tomatoes, an onion and some cheese in the fridge. Pizza was screaming out at me. The secret here is a hot, hot oven so your pizza gets a gorgeously crisp crust. You can buy pizza bases very easily. You can create your own toppings and of course make your own delicious tomato sauce too.

BASIC TOMATO SAUCE FOR PIZZA

MAKES ENOUGH FOR 4 PIZZAS

YOU WILL NEED:

50g/2oz butter
2 garlic cloves, peeled, chopped and crushed
½ onion, chopped finely
600g/1¼lb canned chopped tomatoes
1 teaspoon sugar
1 teaspoon dried oregano

1 Melt the butter in a pan

2 Add the garlic and onions. Cook on a medium heat for 3–4 minutes until soft.

3 Add the tomatoes and the sugar. Season with salt and pepper and add the oregano.

4 On a medium-low heat, cook for up to half an hour to get all the flavours gorgeously intense. Set aside until you're ready to assemble your pizza.

Optional Extras: I often use a red onion instead of a white one as it's just a bit different. You could also add 1 teaspoon of tomato purée, which has a much more concentrated tomato flavour. Also feel free to throw in some fresh tomatoes. I would suggest using 4–6 halved small tomatoes.

Serving Suggestions: Delicious as your base for pizza. Just add a little bit of sliced mozzarella and basil and you have the perfect Italian pizza.

Leftovers: This will keep in an airtight container in the fridge for 3 days. To reheat it, slowly bring it to the boil in a pan.

PIZZA MARGARITA MAKES 4

YOU WILL NEED:

4 pizza bases
8 tablespoons Basic Tomato
  Sauce for Pizza (see opposite)
350g/12oz mozzarella, sliced
  thinly
500g/18oz Cheddar cheese,
  grated
4 teaspoons dried oregano
  (optional)

This is very simple and made with just tomato and cheese. The secret is to use a lot of cheese so that when you take a bite, you end up with cheese strings everywhere. If you don't have four baking trays, you can always flip over some roasting trays and use them instead (see step 2).

Preheat the oven to 200°C/400°F/Gas Mark 6.

2 Place 3–4 slices of mozzarella on each pizza.

3 Then scatter with grated cheese. Season well and if you have it, sprinkle a teaspoon of dried oregano over each pizza.

1 Put the pizza bases on baking trays and spread each one with 2 tablespoons of the gorgeous tomato sauce.

4 Put the pizzas in the hot oven for 15–20 minutes.

You want the pizza base to be golden and crispy, and the cheese should be a little crispy too.

Optional Extras: The list is endless! You could add some ham to the pizza topping, or some pepperoni, mushrooms, black olives, peppers, anchovies…

Serving Suggestions: Having taken it out of the oven, I would serve this with a drizzle of olive oil and maybe a few torn up basil leaves for extra colour and flavour.

Leftovers: I hate reheated pizza as it goes all soggy; however, it's a great snack eaten cold, so leave it in the fridge and eat it for lunch the next day.

MY PERFECT PIZZA MAKES 4

This is my favourite pizza topping. I adore anchovies but I know that a lot of my mates find that weird, so I have left them out, but if you are like me and love them, add 2–3 anchovy fillets to the topping.

YOU WILL NEED:
4 pizza bases
8 tablespoons Basic Tomato Sauce for Pizza (see page 90)
250g/9oz mushrooms, sliced
250g/9oz ham, sliced
350g/12oz mozzarella, sliced thinly
500g/18oz Cheddar cheese, grated
4 teaspoons dried oregano (optional)

Preheat the oven to 200°C/400°F/ Gas Mark 6.

1 Put the pizza bases on baking trays and spread each one with 2 tablespoons of the sauce.

2 Arrange the mushrooms, ham, mozzarella and Cheddar. Scatter with dried oregano, if you're using it..

3 Put them in the hot oven for 15–20 minutes until golden brown and bubbling.

Optional Extras: Anchovies are perfect with this, as are black olives. You could use Parma or Serrano ham instead of the ordinary ham; however they will be more expensive.
Serving Suggestions: Delicious with a drizzle of chilli oil over the top. Make your own by pouring olive oil into a jar with 3–4 sliced red chillies. Leave it for up to a month to mature. Great also with a handful of rocket leaves over the top.

HOT AND SPICY PIZZA

SERVES 4

YOU WILL NEED:

4 pizza bases

8 tablespoons Basic Tomato
Sauce for Pizza (see page 90)

250g/9oz hot pepperoni, sliced

12 slices of preserved red or
green jalapeños, drained

500g/18oz Cheddar cheese,
grated

4 tablespoons chilli oil
(optional)

know that when I have made pizzas for mates in the past they love a
ood spicy version. Therefore this is brilliant to do, especially if you're
making it for boys; you can see how much spice they can take.

Preheat the oven to 200°C/400°F/ Gas Mark 6.

1 Put the pizza bases on baking trays and spread each one with 2 tablespoons of the sauce.

2 Scatter a quarter of the pepperoni slices and the jalapeños over each pizza. Finish off with the cheese and chilli oil, if you're using it.

3 Cook in the oven for 15–20 minutes until golden brown.

Optional Extras: Depends how far you want to go. Feel free to chuck on some more jalapeños.
Serving Suggestion: When it comes out of the oven drizzle the pizza with some more chilli oil.

VEGETARIAN PASTA HEAVEN

SERVES 6

I dedicate this recipe to my friend Greg, who is a devoted vegetarian. When I was much younger he used to come for dinner and I then got experimenting with vegetarian recipes. Whether you're veggie or not, I thoroughly recommend this dish. I started making it when I was 16 and it's always worked wonderfully.

YOU WILL NEED:

1 aubergine, chopped roughly
3 leeks, sliced
4 red onions, quartered
5–6 tablespoons olive oil
3 red peppers, deseeded and chopped roughly
6 tomatoes, quartered
2 sprigs rosemary, thyme, or sage
1kg/2¼lb penne pasta
5 tablespoons chopped parsley
3 garlic cloves, peeled and crushed
100g/3½oz butter
500g/18oz mascarpone

> Preheat the oven to 200°C/400°F/ Gas Mark 6.

> **2** Drizzle with 2 tablespoons of the olive oil. Mix well and roast in the oven for 15 minutes.

1 Put the aubergine, leeks and red onions in a large roasting tray.

3 Add the peppers, tomatoes and herbs to the part-cooked vegetables.

4 Mix well, season with salt and pepper, and add another tablespoon of olive oil if it looks a little dry. Return the roasting tray to the oven for a further 15 minutes.

5 Meanwhile bring a large pan of water to the boil. Add the pasta and simmer for 10 minutes or according to the packet instructions.

6 Mix together the parsley, 3 tablespoons of olive oil and the garlic to make a gorgeous pesto-type sauce.

7 Drain the pasta and return it to the pan. Stir in the butter.

8 Remove the roasted vegetables from the oven and tip them onto the pasta.

9 Stir in the pesto-type sauce and mix well.

10 Season with salt and pepper and stir in the mascarpone. It should taste sensational – creamy, garlicky, and yet full of goodness with the roasted vegetables.

Serve immediately.

Optional Extras: If you want to add some meat I'd suggest some cooked chicken strips, or even some chopped bacon.

Serving Suggestions: Gorgeous with a lovely green salad of lettuce, spring onions and avocado.

Leftovers: The roasted vegetables will keep, covered, in the fridge for 3 days and can be eaten cold in a salad or even as a topping for a pizza. Reheat in the oven at 150°C/300°F/Gas Mark 2 for 15 minutes. The actual pasta dish will keep in the fridge in an airtight container for 3 days. To reheat it, place it in a saucepan over a medium heat for 5–8 minutes and stir in 1 teaspoon of olive oil.

LASAGNE SERVES 6

This is a genuine staple and a truly gorgeous dish. There are three stages to it: the meat sauce, the cheese sauce and then assembling it. Oh, and maybe eating it should be the fourth stage!

Preheat the oven to 200°C/400°F/ Gas Mark 6.

1 Heat the olive oil in a large pan and cook the garlic, onion and chilli over a medium heat. Cook for 5 minutes until soft.

2 Add the mince and cook on a high heat for 3–4 minutes until the mince is brown.

3 Add the ketchup and tomatoes. Season and simmer over a low heat for at least an hour.

4 Meanwhile make the cheese sauce. Put the butter and flour in a pan, and cook on a medium heat, stirring, for 1–2 minutes.

This is called a roux and will help to thicken the sauce.

5 Gradually whisk in the milk. Any lumps should dissolve as the milk becomes thicker. Stir for 4–5 minutes.

6 Taste and season with salt and pepper, then add the cheese. Mix well until the cheese dissolves.

7 Grease a large lasagne dish with butter.

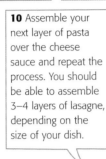

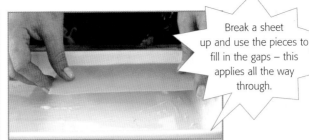

Break a sheet up and use the pieces to fill in the gaps – this applies all the way through.

8 Then lay about 4 pasta sheets on the bottom of the dish.

10 Assemble your next layer of pasta over the cheese sauce and repeat the process. You should be able to assemble 3–4 layers of lasagne, depending on the size of your dish.

9 Spread 3 tablespoons of meat sauce over the pasta and repeat with the cheese sauce.

11 Sprinkle the top with grated cheese.

12 Cook in the oven for 35–45 minutes until golden brown.

Delish!

Optional Extras: You could substitute the meat sauce with roasted vegetables to make a vegetable lasagne. Turn to the recipe for vegetarian pasta heaven (see page 94) for the way to cook them. If you want a bit of extra flavour, add half a teaspoon of grated nutmeg to the cheese sauce along with the milk.

Serving Suggestions: Serve with a delicious green salad or some garlic bread (see page 99).

Leftovers: Lasagne will keep uncooked and assembled in the fridge for 2 days, so you can make it well in advance. Once cooked, it will keep in the fridge for 3 days. To reheat, place in the oven at 150°C/300°F/Gas Mark 2 for 15 minutes, or until piping hot. Use any leftover meat sauce for spaghetti bolognese, or shepherd's pie. Any leftover cheese sauce could be reused in cauliflower cheese (see pages 36–37) or a gooey leek gratin (see page 115).

SPAGHETTI BOLOGNESE

SERVES 6

My dad makes the most sensational spaghetti bolognese. The secret is to let it bubble for as long as possible. The Italians cook it for 3–4 hours and it's even better reheated the next day. Spaghetti bolognese is traditionally a student favourite. I absolutely adore it.

YOU WILL NEED:

4 tablespoons olive oil
4 garlic cloves, peeled and crushed
1 onion, peeled and chopped
1 red chilli, deseeded and chopped
250g/9oz mushrooms, sliced
1kg/2¼lb lean beef mince
2 glasses of red wine
1 tablespoon tomato ketchup
900g/2lb canned tomatoes
2 tablespoons dried oregano (optional)
500g/18oz dried spaghetti
handful grated Cheddar cheese

1 Heat the olive oil in a large saucepan over a medium heat and add the garlic, onion and chilli. Cook for 5 minutes until soft.

2 Add the mushrooms and mince. Season with salt and pepper. Fry on a high heat, for 3–4 minutes until most of the meat is brown but there is still a sign of pink – this will stop it becoming too tough.

3 Add the red wine and ketchup, stirring well, then add the tomatoes and oregano, if you're using it.

4 Let the sauce bubble on a low heat for as long as time allows – ideally at least 1½ hours.

5 Bring a large saucepan of water to the boil and drop in the spaghetti, stirring until it is all submerged. Simmer for 10 minutes, or according to the packet instructions. Drain the pasta then serve it topped with the hot bolognese sauce.

6 Add some grated cheese and eat.

Optional Extras: You could add some bacon for a meatier taste. You could also serve penne pasta with this; mix the cooked penne and bolognese together and place in an ovenproof dish, sprinkled with lots of grated cheese, then place in the oven at 180°C/350°F/Gas Mark 4 for 15 minutes until the cheese is deliciously brown and bubbly.

Serving Suggestions: Serve with some garlic bread (see opposite), a side salad and a glass of red wine.

Leftovers: Bolognese sauce keeps wonderfully well in the fridge for 3 days. To reheat, place in a saucepan and slowly bring to the boil. It also freezes very well for up to 3 months. To defrost, leave it in the fridge overnight and then heat it in a saucepan until piping hot.

GARLIC BREAD SERVES 6

arlic Bread is amazing with lasagne, spaghetti bolognese, or shepherd's
e. It's comfort food at its absolute best and definitely worth the effort.

YOU WILL NEED:

400g/14oz butter, softened
8 garlic cloves, peeled and
  crushed
3 tablespoons parsley, chopped
2 French baguettes

> Preheat the oven to 180°C/ 350°F/Gas Mark 4.

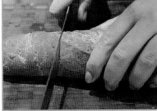

2 Take the baguettes and slice into them at regular intervals along their length. DON'T cut all the way through, however.

3 Fill each pocket with 1 heaped teaspoon of garlic butter.

1 Mix the butter, garlic and parsley together in a bowl. Season with salt and pepper.

> If there is any left over, spread it over the top of the baguettes.

4 Wrap each baguette in foil and place in the hot oven for 15–20 minutes.

Optional Extras: You could use rosemary or even sage if you want an alternative to parsley.
Serving Suggestions: This is an imperative with spaghetti bolognese or lasagne.
Leftovers: Not great, as it does go quite soggy once cooked.

SHEPHERD'S PIE SERVES 6

This is so delicious, especially on winter days. You can have it with some delicious peas and a good glob of ketchup. No clues with the name, but Shepherd's Pie is made with lamb and Cottage Pie with beef, so if you fancy beef then just substitute beef mince for the lamb mince.

YOU WILL NEED:
4 tablespoons olive oil
4 garlic cloves, peeled and crushed
1 red chilli, deseeded and chopped finely
1 red onion, peeled and chopped
3 carrots, peeled and chopped
1kg/2¼lb lean lamb mince
3 tablespoons Worcestershire sauce
2 glasses of red wine
400g/14oz canned chopped tomatoes
250g/9oz Cheddar cheese, grated

Potato Topping:
1.6kg/3½lb potatoes, peeled
110g/4oz butter
200ml/7fl oz milk

Preheat the oven to 200°C/400°F/Gas Mark 6.

1 Heat the olive oil in a large saucepan over a medium heat and add the garlic, chilli, onion and carrots. Cook on a medium to low heat for 4–5 minutes until soft.

2 Up the heat and when the vegetables are soft add the mince.

3 Cook for 4–5 minutes

4 Add the Worcestershire sauce, wine and tomatoes. Season well.

5 Cook for up to 1 hour, longer if you can. It should taste very meaty and delicious.

7 Drain and mash well, add the butter and milk and season with salt and pepper.

6 While the meat is bubbling away, bring a large pan of water to the boil and add the potatoes. Cook until soft, around 15–20 minutes, depending on their size.

8 Spoon in the meat sauce into a large ovenproof dish.

It should half fill the dish.

9 Carefully spoon the mashed potato over the top.

10 Season, then sprinkle with grated Cheddar cheese.

11 Place on a baking tray in the oven for 30–40 minutes until golden and bubbling.

More please!

Optional Extras: You could use Gruyère cheese as a treat for the top, as it's sensational when melted. You could also use celery instead of (or as well as) the carrots.
Serving Suggestions: Amazing with garden peas, ketchup and a glass of red wine.

FISH PIE SERVES 6

I love, love Fish Pie. It's creamy, rich, utterly good comfort food on a plate. There's nothing better, no matter what the season. We were incredibly lucky at Newcastle uni because we were literally 20 minutes away from the coast and everything from oysters to cod was sold at amazing prices. We also had a brilliant fishmonger. The fish was fresh, fresh, fresh! Try and be thrifty with your money and shop around for the best fish. Use markets and fishmongers as they have such a wide and fresh range.

YOU WILL NEED:

- 200g/7oz peeled and ready-cooked prawns
- 4 smoked haddock fillets, skinned and cut into chunks
- 4 cod, haddock, pollock or coley fillets, skinned and cut into chunks
- 3 garlic cloves, peeled and bruised
- 600ml/1 pint milk
- 300ml/10fl oz double cream
- 4 spring onions
- 3 eggs, hard boiled, peeled and sliced (see page 49)
- 4 tablespoons chopped parsley
- 250g/9oz Cheddar cheese, grated

Potato Topping:
- 1.6kg/3½lb potatoes, peeled and chopped
- 110g/4oz butter

Preheat the oven to 180°C/350°F/Gas Mark 4.

1 Bring a large pan of water to the boil and add the potatoes. Cook for 15–20 minutes until very soft.

2 Drain and mash, mix in the butter and season well. Set aside.

Get your fishmonger to skin the fish for you.

The fish should become opaque and a little flaky.

3 Put the prawns and fish in a saucepan with the garlic, milk and cream. Cook on a medium heat for 5–10 minutes until the fish is opaque and cooked through. Taste the sauce and season it with salt and pepper as you like.

4 Use a slotted spoon to remove the fish from the pan and place it in a large ovenproof dish.

5 Slowly bring the milk mixture to the boil. Cook for 3–4 minutes, stirring regularly, until it has thickened a little.

6 Scatter the fish with the spring onions then pour over the sauce.

If it's looking too dry, then feel free to add a little more cream or milk.

7 Arrange the egg slices over the pie. Sprinkle with parsley and season with salt and pepper.

8 Spoon the mashed potato onto the pie, then sprinkle with cheese.

9 Place on a baking tray in the oven for 30–40 minutes until golden and bubbling.

Optional Extras: Feel free to use the kind of fish you like. Cod is very reasonable, as is haddock – I love the smoky flavour of haddock. Salmon is delicious in this as well.

Serving Suggestions: Perfect with green peas, and a bottle of dry white wine, and a whole load of friends.

Leftovers: Since this dish includes ready-cooked prawns in the ingredients, it's not something you should try to keep and then reheat. If you make it without the prawns, however, you can keep it for up to 2 days.

THAI FISHCAKES SERVES 6

Not only fresh and fragrant but also an economical choice, Thai fishcakes are so easy to make and they're great to give your mates. Serve them with some sweet chilli sauce and a big green salad for a healthy and very simple meal. Make sure everyone brings their own booze and get them to chip in for the shopping so the cook or cooks aren't left short-changed.

YOU WILL NEED:

700g/1½lb cod, haddock, or salmon fillets, skinned and chopped

3 spring onions, chopped finely

2 red chillies, deseeded and chopped finely

3 garlic cloves, peeled, chopped and crushed

5cm/2 inches ginger, peeled and chopped finely

3–4 tablespoons finely chopped coriander leaves

3 limes; use the juice of one and grate the zest off them all

1 teaspoon sweet chilli sauce, plus about 200ml/7fl oz extra to serve

2 tablespoons vegetable oil

Chop all the ingredients.

If you have a hand held whizzer you can use it to combine the ingredients even more. A chunkier version is fine, however.

1 Combine the fish, spring onions, chillies, garlic, ginger, coriander, limes and sweet chilli sauce.

2 Take 1 tablespoon of the mixture and shape it into a fishcake using your hands. If the mixture seems too dry add a little more lime juice, and if it's very wet sprinkle about 1 tablespoon of plain flour over your hands to help shape the patties.

You should be able to make about 12 fishcakes from the mixture.

3 Heat the oil in a frying pan and add the fishcakes. You may need to cook them in batches if your pan is small.

4 Fry them over a medium heat for 4–5 minutes on each side until golden. Serve hot.

Serving Suggestions: Sweet chilli sauce is a great dipping sauce, or try soy sauce mixed with a little honey. Great with a big green salad and some boiled potatoes. Perfect for a night in with all your mates.
Leftovers: Cook the fishcakes as soon as you make them or keep them raw in the fridge to cook later that day.

TUSCAN CHICKEN BAKE SERVES 6–8

I did this quite recently for a supper party and it went down a storm.
I love recipes where you just chuck everything in, bung it into the oven
and that's that. Ideal as well if you have people coming for supper, and
then you can just go and get ready when it's all in the oven.

YOU WILL NEED:

- 4 chicken thighs
- 4 chicken legs
- 6 garlic cloves, peeled and bruised
- 4 lemons, quartered
- 4 tablespoons olive oil
- 1 glass of white wine (optional)
- 3 rosemary sprigs, snipped
- 2 red onions, peeled and quartered

Preheat the oven to 180°C/350°F/Gas Mark 4.

2 Squeeze the lemon quarters over the chicken and then tuck the lemon quarters into the dish.

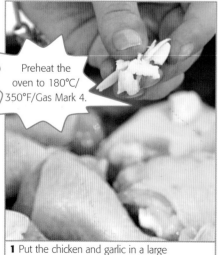

1 Put the chicken and garlic in a large ovenproof dish.

3 Pour over the olive oil. Add the white wine if you're using it.

4 Throw in the rosemary and red onions.

5 Cook in the oven for 20 minutes. Serve hot.

Optional Extras: You could add all sorts of vegetables; tomatoes would be delicious and all sorts of herbs.
Serving Suggestions: To keep with the Italian theme I like to serve this with some pesto (see page 65), gorgeous spaghetti and a salad. It's just so easy.
Leftovers: Keep any leftovers to eat cold in a salad the next day.

7

WASTED
WEEKENDS

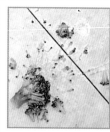

At university, weekends are usually a time for a massive chill out. There's always one highlight of the weekend: the Sunday roast. When the wind is howling and the rain is pouring there is nothing like huddling round a table for a big roast with all the trimmings. Weekends give you time to do this and it can be fun preparing all the bits then chilling out with your mates before you all sit down to eat.

Weekends are also a great time to make stews and casseroles – great whether you're eating in front of the TV or have a few people coming round for dinner. Just cook them in the morning and leave them until you're ready to eat that night.

PERFECT ROAST CHICKEN

SERVES 4

Sweet, juicy and tender roast chicken stuffed with garlic, lemon and a good bit of butter. It's gorgeous with roasted vegetables, but you could also serve it warm with lots of salads in the summer.

YOU WILL NEED:
1.8kg/4lb fresh whole chicken
200g/7oz butter
1 garlic bulb, cut in half horizontally
1 lemon, halved

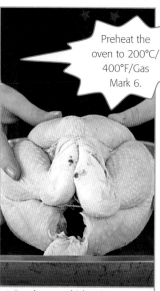

Preheat the oven to 200°C/400°F/Gas Mark 6.

1 Put the raw chicken in a roasting tray.

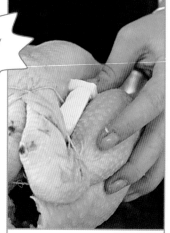

2 Cut the butter into chunks and rub it over the skin on the top of the chicken. Fit some of the butter in the cavities between the legs and the wings.

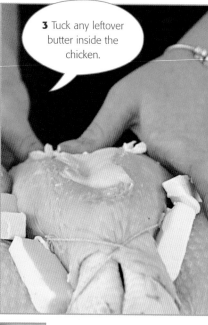

3 Tuck any leftover butter inside the chicken.

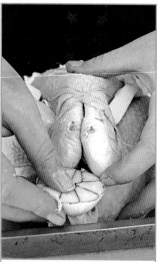

4 Tuck half of the garlic inside the chicken.

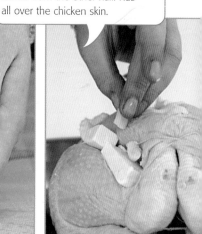

5 Peel and lightly crush the cloves from the other half. Rub all over the chicken skin.

Wash your hands to remove any trace of raw chicken.

6 Tuck a lemon half inside the chicken and squeeze the other half over the outside.

7 Cover the chicken with foil and put it in the hot oven. It will need 20 minutes for every 500g/18oz, plus an additional 20 minutes. So, a 1.8kg/4lb bird will take 1½ hours. Remove the foil after an hour to let the skin brown.

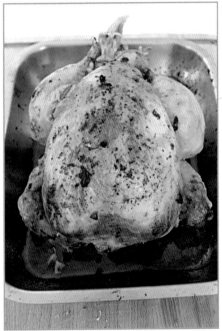

8 Once you have removed the foil, baste the chicken with the cooking juices from time to time. Just spoon them over and quickly return it to the oven.

9 Remove the chicken from the oven and place it on a carving board while you make the gravy (see page 112). Resting it for 10–15 minutes will also make it easier to carve.

Optional Extras: Herbs such as sage, rosemary or thyme are delicious chopped and rubbed all over the buttered skin and stuffed inside the chicken. A glass of white wine is delicious poured into the roasting tray before you place it in the oven. It steams the chicken, keeping it moist, and intensifies the flavours.

Serving Suggestions: Serve with delicious crispy roast potatoes (see page 113), gravy (see page 112) and a selection of vegetables, such as Gooey Leek Gratin (see page 115).

Leftovers: There is so much you can do with roast chicken. Keep the meat and use it in a salad, like Caesar salad (see page 60), or chuck it into a carbonara pasta sauce for a delicious twist on pasta carbonara (see page 29). Use the leftover meat for a sandwich, or even a stir-fry with some noodles. You can keep it in the fridge, covered, for 2 days.

GORGEOUS GRAVY

SERVES 4

A delicious roast chicken requires a really delicious gravy. It only takes a few minutes and can be done while the cooked chicken is resting. I like to add some white wine and use as much of the chicken juices as possible.

YOU WILL NEED:

chicken juices from a roast chicken (see pages 110–111)
2 chicken stock cubes
500ml/18fl oz boiling water
1 glass of white wine
25g/1oz plain flour
25g/1oz butter

2 Crumble the stock cubes into the boiling water and mix well.

1 Take the roasting tray in which you cooked the chicken and carefully pour off any fat. Set the tray on the hob over a medium heat. Mix up all the remaining juices and bits in the tray.

3 Gradually add the stock to the tray and mix well.

4 Add the wine and season with salt and pepper.

7 Pour into a jug and serve.

5 The gravy will be quite thin, so add the flour and butter to thicken it slightly. If you want it really thick, double the amount of flour and butter. Stir well and bring it back to simmering point.

6 Let it bubble for 3 minutes, then taste and season with salt and pepper.

Optional Extras: Add some herbs, such as a couple of rosemary sprigs or thyme, for extra flavour.
Leftovers: I often find myself with some leftover gravy. You can keep it in the fridge for 2 days and reheat it in a saucepan for 5 minutes until piping hot.

INGRID'S ROAST POTATOES SERVES 6

Crispy roast potatoes are a staple part of a roast dinner. They are amazing, but there is an art to getting them right. My best friend makes the best crispy, fluffy roasts and this is the way she does it. They take a while to cook, so remember to start them in plenty of time.

YOU WILL NEED:

8 white potatoes, cut into 5cm/2 inch pieces
4 tablespoons olive oil
50g/2oz butter
2 tablespoons chopped rosemary (optional)

Preheat the oven to 200°C/400°F/Gas Mark 6.

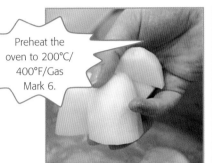

1 Bring a large pan of water to the boil and add the potatoes for 5–8 minutes, until they are beginning to soften.

2 Drain the potatoes and tip them into a large roasting tray.

3 Take a fork and scratch the potatoes, fluffing them up a little.

5 Add the rosemary, if you're using it, and lots of salt.

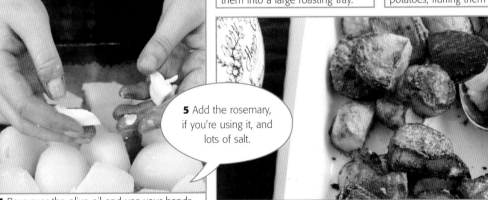

4 Pour over the olive oil and use your hands to rub it in well. Then dot with the butter.

6 Place in the oven to roast for 1½–2 hours until golden and crispy.

Optional Extras: I love cooking these with goose fat. It's a brilliant way to roast potatoes and gets them so crunchy and gorgeous. Just replace the olive oil with goose fat.

Serving Suggestions: Perfect with roast chicken (see pages 110–111) and all the trimmings.

Leftovers: Keep the cooked potatoes and eat them cold in a tuna or chicken salad. They will keep, covered, in the fridge for 2–3 days. To reheat, place in the oven at 130°C/250°F/Gas Mark ½ for 15 minutes.

BUTTERED BROCCOLI

SERVES 6

When I was taught to cook we learnt that vegetables must be seasoned well and treated like everything else; not just drained and served. You want to extract the very best from your ingredients and it's amazing what a little butter, garlic and salt can do.

1 Drop the broccoli into a pan of salted boiling water. Cook for 5–8 minutes until the broccoli are soft when pricked with a knife. (Leave the lid off or they will lose their beautiful colour.)

2 Drain the broccoli and tip them back into the saucepan.

3 Add the butter and garlic, then season well with salt and pepper.

4 Transfer to a serving dish and serve immediately.

Optional Extras: Replace the butter with olive oil if you want a lighter taste. A few pine nuts are amazing scattered on the top of the broccoli.
Serving Suggestions: These can be served with anything from a delicious roast (see pages 110–111) to a shepherd's pie (see pages 100–101) or fish pie (see pages 102–103). Or you could just eat them on their own – still amazing.
Leftovers: Green veg aren't the best when reheated as they turn quite soggy. However, cold broccoli are delicious cold in a salad or with some cold fish.

GOOEY LEEK GRATIN
SERVES 6

YOU WILL NEED:

50g/2oz butter

6 leeks, sliced

300ml/10fl oz double cream

250g/9oz Cheddar cheese, grated

very time I cooked a roast at uni, this dish was always requested. I adore eeks anyway; I think they are versatile and creamy. When combined with ream and cheese and browned off in the oven, they are sensational.

Preheat the oven to 180°C/350°F/Gas Mark 4.

1 Melt the butter in a frying pan, then add the leeks and fry over a medium heat.

2 The leeks will start to separate and shrivel up a little. Cook for 4 minutes until soft and then transfer to a deep ovenproof dish. I use one 20.5cm/8 inches in diameter.

3 Pour over the cream and sprinkle with the cheese.

4 Place in the oven for 15 minutes until the cheese is melted, golden and sensational.

Optional Extras: Use Gruyère cheese for gorgeous added decadence. It's not as reasonable as Cheddar but is heaven when melted.

Serving Suggestions: A bit like cauliflower cheese, this is amazing on its own; however, I adore it with roast chicken (see pages 110–111).

Leftovers: Cover the cooked dish and keep in the fridge for up to 2 days. To reheat, place it in the oven at 130°C/250°F/Gas Mark ½ for 15 minutes until hot.

BEEF STEW SERVES 6

What's not to love about a good hearty beef stew with some amazing mashed potato and red wine? It's also very reasonable to make, as you need to use stewing beef, which is cheap.

YOU WILL NEED:

- 2 beef stock cubes
- 300ml/10fl oz boiling water
- 2 tablespoons olive oil
- 1 onion, peeled and quartered
- 5 garlic cloves, peeled, chopped and crushed
- 700g/1½lb stewing steak, such as chuck or brisket, cut into large chunks
- 2 tablespoons plain flour
- 3 carrots, peeled and sliced
- 3 leeks, sliced
- 2 tablespoons tomato ketchup
- 2–3 glasses of red wine
- 4 rosemary sprigs

Preheat the oven to 170°C/325°F/ Gas Mark 3.

1 Find a large ovenproof casserole dish. If you don't have one, use a large saucepan and just cook it on the hob rather than in the oven. Crumble the stock cubes into the boiling water. Stir and set aside.

2 Heat the oil in the pan. Fry the onion and garlic for 3–4 minutes over a medium heat until soft.

3 Toss the beef in the flour then add it to the pan for 2–3 minutes.

4 Add the carrots and leeks, stir well and season with salt and pepper.

5 Add the tomato ketchup, wine and stock.

6 Mix well and throw in the sprigs of rosemary.

7 Cover with a lid and bung in the hot oven for 2½–3 hours. Alternatively leave on the hob on a low heat for the same amount of time, stirring occasionally.

8 Check the stew after 2½ hours by cutting a piece of the meat in half. If it falls apart easily it's done. Also taste and check the seasoning. Serve hot on a mountain of mash.

Optional Extras: Add some chopped herbs such as sage or rosemary when frying the garlic and onion; that is so good. You could use the same amount of tomato purée if you don't want to use ketchup. Also baby onions are amazing in stews, and instead of an onion you could use 6 baby onions or even shallots peeled and chucked in with the garlic.
Serving Suggestions: Try this with some gorgeous garlic mashed potato (see page 83), and some red wine. So easy.
Leftovers: A cooked beef stew will keep in the fridge for 2–3 days. To reheat it, simply place it back on the hob, bring to the boil and serve piping hot. It's also lovely with boiled potatoes and a green salad.

CHICKEN, BACON AND MUSHROOM CASSEROLE SERVES 6

I have cooked this dish so many times – it's really reliable and so delicious. It was inspired by a recipe I was taught at the Ballymaloe Cookery School and is perfect comfort food.

YOU WILL NEED:
4–5 tablespoons olive oil
6 baby onions or shallots, peeled
5 garlic cloves, peeled and crushed lightly
3 carrots, peeled and chopped
200g/7oz baby button mushrooms
200g/7oz bacon lardons
6 chicken thighs
2 glasses of white wine
500ml/18fl oz boiling water
2 chicken stock cubes
4–6 thyme sprigs

Preheat the oven to 180°C/350°F/ Gas Mark 4.

1 Heat 2 tablespoons of the oil in a large frying pan and throw in the onions and garlic.

2 Cook on a medium heat for 2–3 minutes, then transfer to a large casserole dish or an ovenproof saucepan.

3 Put the frying pan back on the heat and add the carrots. Cook them for 2 minutes until slightly coloured, then add to the casserole.

4 Repeat this process with the mushrooms and then the bacon. If the frying pan gets dry, add some more olive oil.

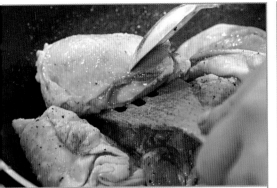

5 Add 2 more tablespoons of oil to the frying pan and add the chicken thighs. Cook for 2 minutes on each side, just give them a golden colour. Transfer to the casserole.

6 Return the frying pan to the heat and heat half the white wine. Be careful as it might spit. Then pour it into the casserole; this is known as de-glazing.

7 Tip the rest of the wine straight into the casserole.

If the sauce is too liquid, transfer 400ml/14fl oz into a saucepan and add 50g/2oz butter and 50g/2oz flour to thicken it. Then tip it back into the casserole.

8 Mix the boiling water with the stock cubes. Tip into the casserole with the thyme. Season well and cook the oven for 45 minutes.

9 Check the chicken is cooked by cutting into the thickest part of the leg or breast. The meat should be white with no obvious signs of pink.

10 Serve now or keep it warm in the oven at 130°C/250°F/Gas Mark ½ for 20 minutes.

Optional Extras: If you wanted to make this a vegetarian casserole, just remove the chicken and bacon and add some red onions, leeks, sugar snap peas and potatoes. Just cook them in the frying pan like you do all other ingredients and transfer to the casserole.

Serving Suggestions: For me there is only one way to eat this – with gorgeous creamy mashed potato (see page 82), and a green salad.

Leftovers: A cooked casserole will keep in the fridge for 3 days. To reheat, simply place it back on the hob, bring to the boil and serve piping hot.

LOTTIE'S CHICKEN AND COCONUT CURRY
SERVES 4–6

My friend Lottie invited quite a few of us round one night and stunned us all with this absolute winner. A recipe for success, it was not only utterly delicious, but it also fuelled us with energy to party into the early hours.

YOU WILL NEED:

4 tablespoons sunflower oil

6 garlic cloves, peeled, chopped finely and crushed

4 spring onions, chopped finely

1 red onion, peeled and chopped finely

3cm/1¼ inch piece of ginger, peeled and chopped

5 tablespoons mild curry paste

6 skinless chicken breasts, sliced into strips

1 red pepper, deseeded and chopped

3 x 400ml/14fl oz cans coconut milk

150ml/5fl oz chicken stock (optional)

200g/7oz frozen peas

1 Heat the oil over a high heat in a large wok or saucepan.

2 Add the garlic, spring onions, red onion and ginger, turn the heat down to medium and fry for 2 minutes.

3 Up the heat a bit to medium-high, stir in the curry paste and fry for 1 minute.

4 Reduce the heat to medium and add the chicken breasts and red pepper, followed by the coconut milk.

5 Bring this to the boil by upping the heat to high. Then reduce the heat to medium again to maintain a steady simmer. Simmer for 7–10 minutes, then check your chicken is cooked by cutting open one of the slices to make sure that it's all white with no sign of pink flesh.

6 Taste, and if it's too intensely coconutty for your liking, add the chicken stock. It's totally up to you.

7 Last, add the frozen peas and cook for 3 minutes until they are soft. Serve immediately.

Optional Extras: Well, you could add some potatoes, or sweet potatoes. Butternut squash would be delicious too.
Leftovers: This will keep in the fridge for up to 2 days. Reheat it slowly in a pan until piping hot, if it seems too dry add 50ml/2fl oz chicken stock. Try serving it with noodles this time (see page 68).
Serving Suggestions: Serve sprinkled with coriander or parsley alongside some basmati rice and maybe some poppadoms, if you wish.

FRAGRANT VEGETABLE CURRY

SERVES 4

Even though I am not a vegetarian, I'm a big fan of vegetable curries. After some playing around with ingredients, I have decided that sweet potatoes are the key to success for this recipe.

YOU WILL NEED:

1 aubergine, chopped into cubes
2 carrots, peeled and sliced
140g/5½ oz green beans
2 sweet potatoes, peeled and chopped into cubes
400ml/14fl oz water
2 tablespoons vegetable oil
1 red onion, peeled and chopped roughly
3 garlic cloves, peeled, finely chopped and crushed
1 green chilli, sliced
2 tablespoons curry paste
2 tablespoons coconut milk
2 tablespoons plain yoghurt
3 tomatoes, quartered
handful of chopped coriander leaves

1 Put the aubergine, carrots, green beans and sweet potatoes in a large saucepan, add the water and bring to the boil .

2 Cover and cook for 5–8 minutes over a medium heat until the vegetables are tender. There won't be enough water to cover all the veg but that's fine. This will steam them more than boil them.

3 Meanwhile heat the oil in a large wok, then add the onion, garlic and chilli and fry on a medium heat till soft.

4 Add the curry paste. Stir well and cook for 2 minutes.

6 Spoon in the coconut milk. Mix well and season with salt and pepper.

5 Add your cooked vegetables, including the cooking water.

7 Add the yoghurt and tomatoes.

8 Cook for a further 2–3 minutes and then throw in the coriander leaves at the end.

Optional Extras: ½ teaspoon of cumin seeds would be gorgeous here. Feel free to replace the vegetables with others that you like better. You could also cook the vegetables in vegetable stock instead of water for more flavour.
Serving Suggestions: Serve with some gorgeous Thai Fragrant Rice (see page 125)
Leftovers: Keep covered in the fridge and eat the following day, perhaps with noodles for a change. To reheat, place in a wok or saucepan and cook for about 5 minutes until piping hot.

HOW TO COOK RICE

SERVES 1

YOU WILL NEED:

75g/3oz basmati rice or long grain rice

This is an easy way to cook rice that will guarantee delicious results – light and fluffy grains that are perfectly cooked every time. Rice is one of those versatile and cheap ingredients, like pasta, which can be kept in your store cupboard and will always come in handy as an accompaniment. Yet it can also be a delicious meal in its own right, with just a few extra bits thrown in. I most often use basmati rice whenever I'm cooking rice. In Hindi it means 'Queen of fragrance' and is delicious with curries. I also adore it just with some butter and coriander. Long grain rice is cooked and prepared in the same way.

1 Bring a large pan of water to the boil and add a pinch of salt.

2 Add the rice and stir well so it doesn't stick.

3 Cook for 10–12 minutes until soft. Test a few grains to check.

4 Drain and serve immediately.

BUTTERED BASMATI WITH CORIANDER SERVES 4

Never associate simplicity with lack of taste or flavour. I could eat bowls of rice cooked like this. Just two extra ingredients add so much flavour.

Optional Extras: If you're not a fan of coriander, which I know many aren't, then use flat-leaf parsley instead.
Serving Suggestions: Serve with a delicious curry or even a casserole.
Leftovers: It is dangerous to reheat rice, so make sure you use it all up.

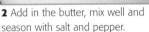

1 Cook the rice as shown opposite.

2 Add in the butter, mix well and season with salt and pepper.

3 Scatter with the coriander and mix well

THAI FRAGRANT RICE SERVES 4

I love this rice, it's sensual and such good food. Similar to basmati, it is slightly stickier. It would be delicious with curry, or you could just serve it with some vegetables and soy sauce for a delicious dish in its own right.

YOU WILL NEED:
1 litre/1¾ pints boiling water
350g/12oz Thai jasmine rice
juice of ½ lime

Serving Suggestions: Serve with oriental dishes, such as Prawn and Coconut Stir-fry (see page 70).

1 Boil the water in a large pan and add the rice. Stir well so the grains do not stick.

2 Cook for 10 minutes until the rice is soft, then drain it through a colander.

3 Tip the rice into a serving bowl and squeeze over the lime juice.

AFRICAN BROWN RICE

SERVES 4

YOU WILL NEED:

300g/11oz basmati rice

2 tablespoons vegetable oil

1 onion, peeled and chopped finely

4 garlic cloves, peeled and chopped finely

200g/7oz bacon lardons

4 tablespoons soy sauce

3 tablespoons currants or raisins

I have been lucky to visit Portugal quite often. They cook so beautifully and it's interesting learning about and tasting foreign food. There's always something I pick up that I then cook back at home. This is a very simple rice dish from a superb restaurant called Dos Passos in the Algarve. I spent a morning in their kitchen and was taught how they make it.

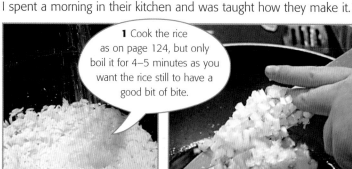

1 Cook the rice as on page 124, but only boil it for 4–5 minutes as you want the rice still to have a good bit of bite.

2 Drain the rice, run it under cold water for 2 minutes and set aside.

3 Heat the oil in a large saucepan and add the onion and garlic. Cook on a medium-low heat for 15 minutes until they are very soft.

4 Up the heat and add the bacon. After a minute reduce the heat back to medium-low and cook for 10 minutes.

5 Tip in the rice and stir well, mixing everything together. Then add the soy sauce and stir well. The rice will turn light brown.

6 Cook on a medium heat for 15 minutes, as you want the saltiness of the soy to evaporate.

7 At the end, throw in the currants or raisins and serve.

Optional Extras: I wouldn't add anything extra here, as this is how the Portuguese do it and it's the best.
Serving Suggestions: Serve with something simple like some grilled chicken or fish. It's very rich, so you wouldn't want it with anything too strong.
Leftovers: Rice shouldn't be reheated, so keep eating.

SPECIAL FRIED RICE SERVES 4

This is great for using up all sorts and emptying the fridge of random bits that you're not sure where or how to use. My mum calls it a 'whip round the fridge' night when she cooks this up.

YOU WILL NEED:
- 300g/11oz long grain or basmati rice
- 2 tablespoons olive oil
- 200g/7oz bacon lardons
- 1 onion, chopped
- 2 garlic cloves, peeled, finely chopped and crushed
- 200g/7oz cooked chicken, beef or lamb leftovers
- 200g/7oz frozen peas

1 Cook the rice as shown on page 124.

4 Throw in the chicken, beef or lamb.

2 Heat the oil in a frying pan and add the bacon, onion and garlic. Fry until the bacon is golden.

3 Drain the rice and throw it in the pan with the onion and bacon, mixing well. Season with salt and pepper.

6 Mix everything together and serve – it's as easy as that.

5 Add the peas and cook for a further 4–5 minutes, stirring.

Optional Extras: Add some chopped parsley, for a bit more green. A nice sliced red chilli would be delicious and would also give it a real kick. 1 tablespoon sweet chilli sauce added along with the peas would be gorgeous too.
Serving Suggestions: Amazing on its own with a salad. Great as well with some roasted chicken or stir-fried vegetables.
Leftovers: Do not reheat rice.

8 | HOUSE PARTIES

House parties are a brilliant opportunity to get everyone together for a big feast and the ultimate party. At uni, everyone jumps at the invite to a house party, but make sure that they bring some booze and even food if you like.

The recipes in this chapter are for eight or more, although you could double or even triple the quantities if needed. It's great to have a huge bowl of curry and just watch everyone dig in. Also I'm a major fan of barbecues whatever the season; I often do one around Hallowe'en, when everyone can go outside in the garden (providing it's not raining) to scoff hot sausages and mulled wine. The perfect winter evening!

CHILLI CON CARNE SERVES 8

A hot and warming chilli con carne is quite simply an ultimate favourite and perfect for a house party when feeding the masses. I love a good bit of spice, so chillies and chilli flakes are brill in this. Whack it on the table when you're done and just watch the bun fight as everyone rushes over. Great with a cold beer or some red wine.

Finely chop the onions, garlic and chillies.

2 Add the chilli flakes. Cook gently for 3–4 minutes

You should be hit with the smells of the garlic and spice – all great.

1 Heat the olive oil in a frying pan on a medium heat. Add the red onions, garlic and fresh chillies.

3 Turn the heat right up and add the beef mince. Season well and cook until brown.

4 Reduce the heat to medium and add the tomatoes, red wine, Worcestershire sauce and Tabasco sauce. Stir well and then add the kidney beans.

6 Serve hot with a dollop of soured cream.

5 Simmer for as long as time allows. I like this to simmer for at least an hour, as all the flavours really intensify. Taste it after an hour and adjust the seasoning accordingly.

Need a bigger bowl.

I can feed myself, you know.

Optional Extras: Don't add the Tabasco sauce if you don't like it too hot, but it does give it a real kick. Chopped parsley or coriander would be brilliant at the end, sprinkled over.
Serving Suggestions: I like this with rice and some soured cream, Guacamole (see page 78) and maybe a side salad. It's so easy to do for large numbers.
Leftovers: Never throw away any leftover chilli; it's excellent the next day, as it just seems to get better and better. It's great reheated slowly in a saucepan until hot and then served in a jacket potato with grated cheese. Recovery food.

MY ULTIMATE THAI GREEN CURRY SERVES 6–8

I have requests for this when my mates are hungover or, weirdly, when they have a cold. Fragrant Thai food with a little spice really clears blocked noses, and is just so comforting. This is also perfect food to do when you have lots of people round as, like chilli, you can place it on the table with some rice and just let everyone tuck in.

YOU WILL NEED:

4 tablespoons vegetable oil
4 garlic cloves, peeled and chopped finely
1 x 2cm/¾ inch ginger, peeled and chopped finely
4 spring onions, sliced
3 lemongrass stalks, peeled and chopped finely
2 green chillies, deseeded and chopped finely
grated zest and juice of 6 limes
4 tablespoons Thai green curry paste
1kg/2¼lb chicken breasts or pieces, sliced
1.2 litres/2 pints coconut milk (3 x 400ml cans)
1 chicken stock cube
200ml/7fl oz boiling water
600g/1¼lb fresh green beans, topped and tailed
2 handfuls of torn coriander

1 Heat the oil in a frying pan over a medium heat. Add the garlic, ginger, spring onions, lemongrass and chillies. Stir-fry for 3–4 minutes until they are soft.

2 Up the heat and add the lime zest and juice.

3 Stir in the curry paste.

4 Stir-fry for 3 minutes then add the chicken.

7 Simmer for 5 minutes until the chicken is cooked.

6 Mix the stock cube into the boiling water. Pour into the pan.

5 Stir the chicken round well, then add the coconut milk immediately.

8 Then add in the green beans and cook for a further 5 minutes.

Check the chicken is cooked by cutting open a slice to make sure there is no sign of pink flesh.

9 Scatter with coriander and serve.

Optional Extras: Green peppers would work very well instead of the green beans, and if you want it not to be so green you could use red chillies instead of green.

Serving Suggestions: This is great if you're feeding a crowd. Serve it with some boiled rice, or even just some poppadoms. If you're eating this in a smaller group, noodles would be amazing.

Leftovers: Put any leftovers in an airtight container and keep for up to 2 days in the fridge or for up to 3 months in the freezer. To reheat, defrost thoroughly and reheat gently in a saucepan until piping hot.

VODKA WATERMELON

SERVES 8 OR MORE

This is such fun, and perfect for a house party. Watermelon is at its best and is also most available during the summer.

2 Knife out the flesh at the top of the incision. Use a spoon to dig a hole as far down to the centre as you can.

1 Take the watermelon and using a knife carefully cut a hole about 5cm/2 inches wide.

3 Pour the vodka into the hole, put the watermelon 'lid' back on and leave for an hour.

Watch out, it's stronger than you think…

5 Then you can cut it open and eat all the melon, which will have soaked up all the remaining vodka.

4 When your mates come round, grab a whole lot of straws and sip up the melon-y vodka.

CRACKING COSMOPOLITAN COCKTAIL
SERVES 1

YOU WILL NEED:

50ml/2fl oz vodka

30ml cranberry juice

juice of 1 lime

This is a great cocktail and perfect with the lime and chilli prawn kebabs (see page 138). It has a little lime juice in it, which enhances the lime in the prawns. It's also pink, punchy and fun.

YUM! Perfect for a cracking party mood.

1 Pour the vodka into a large glass and add the cranberry and lime juices.

BARBECUE SELECTION

At uni, the start of summer is obviously a fun time; however, it means one thing: EXAMS. Everyone is in need of a good dinner and de-stress after days of endless revision. So why not have a small house party and do a barbecue? Chicken thighs, kebabs and sausages are all great for lifting the mood, especially with a cheeky cocktail to wash it all down. Don't feel you have to limit barbecues to the summer. I always do one on Hallowe'en, then have loads of mates round along with some mulled wine and sausages in the garden. Whatever the occasion, these are great for a cheap, relaxed party night at home.

SAUSAGES

A barbecue staple, and so, so delicious with a bit of ketchup. Don't save them just for summer, they're gorgeous in winter too, and great for a Hallowe'en party. Cocktail sausages would be scrumptious here too.

YOU WILL NEED:
16 sausages
4 tablespoons runny honey
2 tablespoons sesame seeds
(optional)

Preheat a barbecue.

Turn them over half way through.

1 Place the sausages in a dish and pour over the runny honey. Mix well.

2 Place the sausages on the barbecue and cook over the hot coals for 10 minutes until golden brown.

3 Put the cooked sausages in a bowl and sprinkle with the sesame seeds, if you're using them. If they don't stick very well, drizzle in another tablespoon of honey.

Tuck in.

Optional Extras: Sausages are amazing on their own, so if you don't want to add the honey or sesame seeds then just cook them without. I just love the stickiness that comes from the honey. Wrap a rasher of bacon around each sausage for an extra meat fest.
Serving Suggestions: Dip in lots of ketchup and mustard.
Leftovers: These are great eaten cold, and can be kept in the fridge, covered, for 2 days. To reheat, place in a pan and cook for 5 minutes until hot. Have a sausage sandwich to nurse away the hangover after your party.

HONEY AND MUSTARD CHICKEN

SERVES 10

YOU WILL NEED:

10 chicken thighs, drumsticks or wings
3 tablespoons runny honey
3 tablespoons mustard

Any barbecue would be incomplete without barbecued chicken. This marinade gives the meat a delicious sweet-savoury edge that tastes amazing with the smoky flavours from the barbecue.

3 Use your hands to rub the mixture all over the chicken.

1 Place all the chicken pieces in a large dish.

2 Smother with honey and mustard.

If you're making this in advance, which is always great whenever you marinate something, put it in the fridge for 30 minutes. Or even better, make it in the morning and keep it in the fridge all day so the flavours of the honey and mustard have more time to soak into the meat.

4 When your barbecue is hot, put the chicken on it, turning every 3 minutes. Cook for about 10 minutes until they are crispy, golden brown and cooked through. To check that they are thoroughly cooked, cut one open – there should be no sign of pink flesh, just white chicken meat.

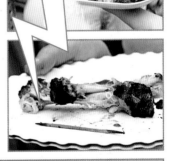

Optional Extras: To spice up the marinade a little, add some hot chilli sauce, or even a finely chopped red or green chilli. Herbs such as rosemary, chopped finely and rubbed onto the chicken, would also be delicious.

Serving Suggestion: Staple barbecue sauces of course: ketchup, mayonnaise, barbecue sauce. Serve along with other barbecue classics, such as sausages, burgers and salad.

LIME AND CHILLI PRAWN KEBABS

SERVES 10

These are so pungent and a real tasty treat. Supermarkets do great deals on ready cooked and peeled prawns and they are often quite an economical treat. As always with fish, if you are near to a fishmonger, pop in to weigh up the prices of some little cooked and peeled prawns against the supermarkets.

YOU WILL NEED:
- 300g/10oz cooked and peeled prawns
- juice of 3 limes
- 2 red chillies, deseeded and finely chopped
- 2 tablespoons soy sauce
- 20 wooden cocktail sticks or skewers

Soak the cocktail sticks or skewers in water – this prevents them from burning on the barbecue.

This is great if left to marinate in the fridge for a few hours, but if you're short of time then 10–30 minutes is better than nothing.

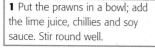

1 Put the prawns in a bowl; add the lime juice, chillies and soy sauce. Stir round well.

Don't forget that since the prawns have already been cooked, you're not trying to cook them, just crisp them up and warm them through.

2 Thread the prawns onto the pre-soaked cocktail sticks or skewers.

3 Spoon over any remaining juices at the bottom of your bowl and then place the kebabs on the barbecue for 5 minutes.

Serving Suggestions: So good dipped in some soy sauce or even some sweet chilli sauce, or just squeeze some lime juice over them before serving and you're away.

BARBECUED BANANAS SERVES 10

If you're having a barbecue, this is a sensational and ridiculously simple dessert. Just whack the whole bananas on the barbecue, slit them open and fill them with a variety of fillings. Delish…

YOU WILL NEED:

10 bananas

Filling options:

10 tablespoons sugar

300g/11oz milk or dark chocolate, broken into pieces

You don't want it red hot or the skin of the bananas will blister.

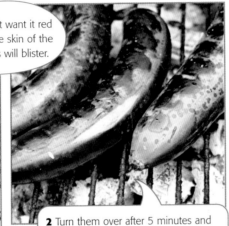

1 Place the whole bananas on a barbecue that has been used and therefore is just cooling down.

2 Turn them over after 5 minutes and the skin should be black. Don't panic, this is what you're looking for.

3 After another 5 minutes both sides should be black and the bananas might be bubbling a little through the skin. Remove them from the barbecue.

Eat immediately. Amazing!

4 Slit the bananas open lengthways and gently pull them open, leaving the skin intact.

5 Divide the chocolate between the bananas and sprinkle with the sugar.

Optional Extras: this is one of those dishes that are very personal; everyone always seems to have their own favourite combinations. You could add marshmallows, 1 tablespoon of cream per banana or 1 tablespoon of custard in each one – it's up to you.

Serving Suggestions: A scoop of ice cream would be amazing with these bananas. Hot and cold together – yum. Don't hang about though, eat the bananas while they're still warm.

Leftovers: It would be a worry if there were any left!

THE ULTIMATE HOT CHOCOLATE

SERVES 1

When I was at school I had a coffee shop that was my saviour and I went there a few days a week after school for one of their epic hot chocolates. Marshmallows in hot chocolate – whoever came up with that is a hero!

YOU WILL NEED:

1 tablespoon cocoa powder, plus extra to decorate

300ml/10fl oz milk

4 tablespoons double cream, whipped

small handful of marshmallows

1 Take a large mug and spoon in the cocoa powder.

2 Gently heat your milk in a pan.

3 When the milk is hot pour it into the mug with the cocoa powder, stirring all the time.

4 Whisk the cream.

Keep whisking until it's nice and thick.

5 When it's thick and stiff spoon it on top of the chocolate drink.

6 Push in the marshmallows

7 Dust with a bit of cocoa powder.

Fancy another?

Optional Extras: A teaspoon of whisky would be gorgeous and give this a real kick.
Serving Suggestions: Drink on its own, or with some lovely chocolate to nibble on while you chill out and chat.

9

TIFF'S TREATS

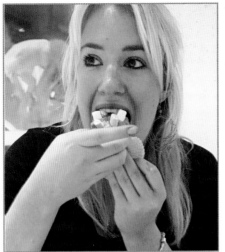

If you've got a sweet tooth, this is the chapter for you – a selection of my much-loved home puddings. I've also added some irresistible sweet bites, such as chocolate brownies and cute cupcakes that are perfect to grab and go. Cakes have a reputation for being a bit tricky, but all these recipes are really easy, so you might feel a bit of a fraud when your friends tell you how impressed they are. Say nothing and just accept the compliments! There's something in here for everyone: a gorgeous birthday cake that would be even better than an actual present; a comforting hot apple crumble; and a banana bread that's ideal for the occasional tea break, or in my case not so occasional.

BRILLIANT CHOCOLATE BROWNIES

MAKES 20 MEDIUM SIZE BROWNIES

YOU WILL NEED:

225g/8oz butter, plus
  2 tablespoons for greasing
275g/10oz dark or milk
  chocolate, broken into pieces
4 medium eggs
275g/10oz muscovado sugar
200g/7oz plain flour
½ teaspoon baking powder

The secret here is the brown sugar, which makes the brownies go ever so gooey and soft. A brownie should have a crispy top and then a gorgeous squidgy centre. These hit the spot perfectly.

Preheat the oven to 180°C/350°F/ Gas Mark 4.

1 Grease a 30cm/12 inch x 20cm/8 inch baking tin with butter. Line it with greaseproof paper.

2 Melt the chocolate and butter in a saucepan until they make a smooth mixture. Set aside to cool for a few minutes.

3 Beat the eggs in a bowl and mix in the muscovado sugar.

4 Add the chocolate mixture and stir well.

5 Gently add the flour and baking powder, stirring until evenly mixed.

6 Pour the mixture into the lined tin and cook in the hot oven for 25 minutes.

7 Remove from the oven. It should have a wonderful crisp top yet the muscovado sugar will have made it sensationally gooey in the middle.

8 Cut into squares (you choose the size) and serve.

Optional Extras: I'm not a great fan of nutty brownies, but if you like them, feel free to add a handful of walnuts when you add the flour. You could of course use caster sugar instead of muscovado sugar.

Serving Suggestions: Serve as a delicious afternoon treat, or even as a pudding with some vanilla ice cream. Mini brownies are great if you've got lots of friends coming round.

Leftovers: These will keep for 3 days in an airtight container.

CHOCOLATE MOUSSE **SERVES 6–8**

I make this mousse with egg white rather than cream, as it's healthier and also gives it an incredibly light and fluffy texture. Pour it into wine glasses or tumblers, put them in the fridge to set and then top with some fresh fruit. Seriously easy, yet surprisingly impressive.

YOU WILL NEED:

350g/12oz milk chocolate, broken into chunks

4 medium eggs

150g/5oz butter

75g/3oz caster sugar

150g/5oz blueberries

1 Melt the chocolate by putting it in a heatproof bowl over a pan of simmering water. Stir as it melts; this should take 3–4 minutes.

2 The bowl should fit snugly, but it mustn't touch the water. Leave the melted chocolate to cool for 5 minutes.

3 Meanwhile, take 2 bowls and separate the eggs.

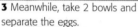

To do this, crack each egg open and allow the white to fall out while you keep the yolk in the shell. Tip the yolk gently between each shell half and let the rest of the egg white drop into the bowl. Tip the yolk into the second bowl. Repeat this process with the remaining eggs.

4 Beat the egg yolks with the melted chocolate. Then stir in the butter and sugar.

The whites should have stiff peaks.

Do this gently or else all the air will be beaten out of your egg whites and you'll be left with a flat mousse.

5 Whisk the egg whites in a large scrupulously clean bowl for 3–5 minutes. An electric whisk would take about 2 minutes.

6 Gently fold the egg whites into the chocolate mixture.

7 Divide the mixture into bowls or glasses. Then leave to set in the fridge for 1–2 hours.

8 Top with blueberries and serve.

Optional Extras: You could whisk some passion fruit into the mousse. This works a treat with white chocolate mousse. Use whatever type of chocolate you like. I love milk, but dark chocolate is very popular as is white chocolate.

Serving Suggestions: Try strawberries or raspberries instead of blueberries.

Leftovers: The set mousse will keep in the fridge for 2–3 days. Always eat chilled.

APPLE CRUMBLE

SERVES 4–6

My grandmother makes a sensational apple crumble so I've stolen all her ideas. It's such a simple pudding and there are never any leftovers.

YOU WILL NEED:

5 large cooking apples (Bramley apples are ideal), peeled, cored and quartered
300ml/10fl oz water
1 teaspoon lemon juice
2 tablespoons granulated sugar

Crumble Topping:
275g/10oz plain flour
175g/6oz granulated sugar
200g/7oz butter, roughly cubed

Preheat the oven to 180°C/350°F/ Gas Mark 4.

1 Put the apples in a pan with the water, lemon juice and sugar. Cover with a lid and cook on a medium heat for 15 minutes until soft. Taste and if they are a little sharp add a bit more sugar. If they're too sweet add another squeeze of lemon juice.

It will transform into a golden crumble, rather like lumpy sand.

2 Meanwhile prepare the crumble topping.

3 Mix the flour and sugar together in a large bowl. Add the butter and use your hands to rub it into the flour. Be patient, the crumble will come together eventually.

5 Put in the oven for 30–40 minutes until golden brown.

4 Spread the apples across the base of an ovenproof dish (I use one 30cm/11 inches x 17cm/6.5 inches), then sprinkle the crumble over the top.

Optional Extras: You could add some raisins, blackberries, raspberries, nutmeg or even vanilla essence to the saucepan of apples. You could also swap the granulated sugar for brown sugar in the crumble mixture.
Serving Suggestions: Serve with a good dollop of vanilla ice cream or custard.
Leftovers: If you have any leftovers then your mates are mad. Keep in the fridge for up to 3 days and reheat in the oven for 10 minutes on 150°C/300°F/Gas Mark 2.

BANANA BREAD

SERVES 6

This cake is perfect tea break material when you've got lots of work. Reward yourself with a slice of delicious banana bread and a cup of tea.

YOU WILL NEED:

75g/3oz butter
175g/6oz caster sugar
450g/1lb bananas, peeled
2 medium eggs
200g/7oz self raising flour
¼ teaspoon bicarbonate of soda
½ teaspoon salt

Preheat the oven to 180°C/350°F/ Gas Mark 4.

2 In a bowl beat together the butter and sugar. Chop the bananas and mash them into the mixture. Add the eggs and combine well.

3 Mix the flour, bicarbonate of soda and salt together in a bowl.

1 Grease a 900g/2lb loaf tin with butter, then line it with a sheet of greaseproof paper.

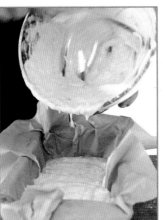

4 Sieve the flour mixture into the banana and butter mixture and mix well until evenly combined.

5 Pour into the loaf tin and put it in the oven for 25 minutes until risen and golden brown.

Optional Extras: Walnuts are delicious. Add them at the same time as the bananas, but make sure no one eating it suffers from a nut allergy.
Serving Suggestions: Eat warm, perhaps spread with a little bit of butter.
Leftovers: This will keep in an airtight container for 3 days.

CUTE CUPCAKES

MAKES ABOUT 20

Cupcakes have become very trendy and are everywhere – there are even shops dedicated entirely to cupcakes. They're perfect when you have lots of friends round and they're really easy to whip up.

YOU WILL NEED:

225g/8oz self raising flour
225g/8oz caster sugar
225g/8oz butter
3 large eggs
20 cupcake cases

Butter Icing:

350g/12oz icing sugar
275g/10oz butter, softened
1 teaspoon pink food colouring
   (optional)
selection of mini marshmallows,
   silver balls or sweets, to
   decorate

Preheat the oven to 180°C/350°F/ Gas Mark 4.

1 In a large bowl, mix together the flour, caster sugar and butter until smooth and evenly combined.

2 Add the eggs and mix well.

The mixture should be light and fluffy.

4 Bake in the oven for 15–20 minutes until golden. To check whether they're cooked, insert a skewer into a cake – if it comes out clean it's cooked, if not give it another 5 minutes. Remove from the oven to cool.

3 Put the cupcake cases on a baking tray and spoon 1 tablespoon into each one.

I love adding food colourings to the icing, as it's fun to have different coloured cupcakes. So add the colour you want.

5 Meanwhile, make the butter icing. Mix the icing sugar with the butter. It's very sweet, so you could always do half butter and half cream cheese if you prefer.

6 Spread the icing over the cupcakes.

7 Decorate with mini marshmallows, silver balls, sweets… It's up to you.

Optional Extras: You could add 1 teaspoon of vanilla essence to the cake mixture. You could also add 2 tablespoons of cocoa and make chocolate cupcakes. This would work in both the cake mixture and the icing.
Serving Suggestions: I love the cakes with different toppings. Get creative!
Leftovers: Un-iced cakes will keep for 3–4 days in an airtight container. If they are iced they need to go into the fridge.

OMA'S UPSIDE DOWN PINEAPPLE CAKE
SERVES 6

YOU WILL NEED:
150g/5oz butter
150g/5oz caster sugar
1 tablespoon/15ml golden syrup or honey (optional)
2x 220g/7½ oz cans pineapple slices (not chunks)
50g/2oz glacé cherries
110g/4oz self raising flour
2 medium eggs, beaten

Oma, my grandmother, is making a huge feature in this book, but her recipes are totally extraordinary. This is easy peasy, and canned pineapples are really cheap and readily available. This would be perfect after a student Sunday lunch, or just after a weekday dinner.

Preheat the oven to 170°C/325°F/Gas Mark 3.

1 Find a baking tin about 23cm/9in across and 4cm/1½in deep. A springform tin would be ideal. Grease the tin with 25g/1oz of the butter.

2 Sprinkle in 25g/1oz of the caster sugar.

3 Drizzle in the golden syrup or honey. This is just delicious, but don't panic if you don't have any, it's fine to leave it out.

4 Arrange the pineapple rings in the dish. Don't throw away the pineapple juice as you may need it later. Fill any holes with bits of pineapple. Put the glacé cherries inside the pineapple rings.

5 In a separate bowl, cream together the remaining butter and caster sugar.

6 Tip in the self raising flour and make a well for the eggs, then beat well.

7 The mixture should have a good spreading consistency. If it seems too dry, however, add 1–2 tablespoons of the pineapple juice.

8 Spread the batter evenly over the pineapples and bake for 20 minutes.

9 Remove the tin from the oven and insert a skewer into the sponge. If your skewer comes out clean, then the pudding is ready, if not, put it back in the oven for a further 5–10 minutes before testing again. When ready, the sponge should be firm and golden. Leave it to cool for 5–10 minutes.

10 Remove the sides of the tin, put a plate upside down over the sponge and flip your pudding onto the plate. The pineapples will be on top and the sponge on the bottom.

Now tuck in.

Leftovers: The cake will keep in an airtight container, such as a biscuit tin, for 3–4 days.

Serving Suggestions: Delicious with ice cream, cream and custard. If you don't want to use pineapples, you could use pears or plums. You could also add 2 tablespoons of cocoa powder to the batter to make a chocolate sponge – this is delicious with pears. You can also cook the pudding in the morning, put it in the fridge and then bung it back in the oven for 5–10 minutes at 150°C/300°F/Gas Mark 2 just before you want to serve it.

BIRTHDAY CAKE SERVES 6

Friends often ask me how to make a simple sponge birthday cake. This is a great recipe and very swift to whip up.

> Preheat the oven to 180°C/350°F/ Gas Mark 4.

1 Beat the butter and sugar together in a large bowl. Then add the eggs and mix well.

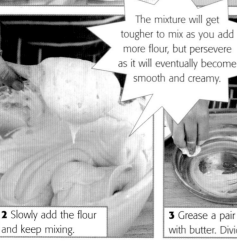

> The mixture will get tougher to mix as you add more flour, but persevere as it will eventually become smooth and creamy.

2 Slowly add the flour and keep mixing.

3 Grease a pair of 22cm/8½ inch cake tins with butter. Divide the mixture between them.

> This is the best bit.

4 Bake in the oven for 20 minutes until golden brown.

> Check they are cooked by inserting a skewer. It's ready if it comes out clean.

5 Remove from the oven, set aside for 5 minutes then turn out onto a board or plate.

6 While the cakes cool, make the icing by beating the butter until smooth and then mixing in the icing sugar.

7 When the cakes are cool, spread the icing over one of the sponges. Spread the other sponge with jam and sandwich the two together.

8 Sift the icing sugar over the top of the cake.

Happy birthday!

Optional Extras: You could decorate the cake with some fresh fruit, chocolate sprinkles or sweets. There are so many bits you can buy for cake decorating, it just depends how far you want to go.

Serving Suggestions: I love decorating my cake with strawberries in the summer, it looks so pretty. In the winter, go for blackberries. Maltesers are also very gorgeous.

Leftovers: The cake will keep in an airtight container in the fridge for 1–2 days but not for much longer, as it will become soggy from the filling.

INDEX

EDITORIAL DIRECTOR Anne Furniss
ART DIRECTOR Helen Lewis
PROJECT EDITOR Katey Mackenzie
PHOTOGRAPHER Claire Peters
DESIGNER Katherine Case
PRODUCTION Vincent Smith,
Aysun Hughes

First published in 2009 by
Quadrille Publishing Limited
Alhambra House, 27–31 Charing Cross Road,
London WC2H 0LS
www.quadrille.co.uk

Text © 2009 Tiffany Goodall
Photography © 2009
Quadrille Publishing Limited
Design and layout © 2009 Quadrille Publishing Limited

Cataloguing-in-Publication Data: a catalogue record for this
book is available from the British Library.

ISBN 978 184400 733 2

Printed in China

ACKNOWLEDGEMENTS

My love of food and cooking began at the famous and truly magical Ballymaloe Cookery School. Darina Allen is one of the most knowledgeable people I have ever met. Thank you for sharing your excitement about food; it is infectious. Rachel Allen, thank you for being a wonderful teacher too. My memories of my time there are so special.

Another big thank you goes to the amazing Martin Blunos for believing in me and all my ideas whilst we worked together for Mark and Spencers in deepest Derby. You generously introduced me to your, and now my agent Rosemary Melbourne. Rosemary, thank you for your solid belief that this would work, and for always being ahead of the game in every way. You have made so much possible for me – thank you. Without your introduction, I would never have met my incredible literary agents, Heather Holden Brown and Elly James. Thank you both for believing in the book and teaching me so much about the world of books and publishing. Elly, your constant support and our brainstorming sessions have been such a laugh.

A huge thank you to everyone at Quadrille. You have made me and my book feel very special and have worked so hard to make it unique. Anne Furniss, thank you for your faith in this project from day one. Helen Lewis, a big thank you for your creative ideas and for putting together an amazingly talented duo in the form of Katherine Case, a brilliant designer, and Claire Peters – I'm so excited to have been part of your first photography project. I know there will be more to come, the photos are beautiful. I am hugely grateful to my wonderful editor, Katey Mackenzie, who has worked tirelessly and has provided many giggles too.

There is a little fish and chip shop in Fulham which is where I learned all about hard work from aged 16 onwards. 'Fishers', do the best fish and chips in the world but also where I have a small family in the like of Gary, Alan, Tom, Danny who I love.

Thank you to ALL of my wonderful friends. There are too many of you to thank but you have all been so supportive. Cress and Char for being there since Barbie days, Ingrid for coming to Chester and always being 100% supportive, and Bex for your pivotal role in Tiff's Tuesdays. A huge thank you to the famous five, you know who you are, for always wanting and encouraging Tiff's Tuesdays. Guy, you've been wonderful but especially at being a great guinea pig.

Betina, thank you for your support.

Oma, you are my inspiration and thank you for giving me so many cooking and recipe ideas and supplying some of your recipe secrets for the book.

My sisters, George and Kamillie; I think you are both budding young chefs. Mama if it hadn't been for you I would never have gone to Ballymaloe, you gave up your kitchen to me for filming, endless photos and an office. Thank you for *everything*, too much to mention here. Papa, you're always there, always supportive and always enthusiastic, thank you.